SECRETS
OF A
PET NANNY

With best wishes

Eileen Riley

SECRETS

OF A

PET NANNY

A journey from the
White House to the Dog House

Eileen Riley

First published 2013 by
Elliott and Thompson Limited
27 John Street, London WC1N 2BX
www.eandtbooks.com

ISBN: 978-1-90965-322-1
Text © Eileen Riley 2013

Some names and other details have been changed to protect
the privacy of individuals, both humans and dogs.

A catalogue record for this book is available from the British Library.

Jacket design: Anna Morrison
Typesetting: MacGuru Ltd
Illustrations: Jay French Studios

Printed in the UK by TJ International Ltd.

For my parents, James and Frances Riley.
Thank you for letting me go, but you knew I never really left.

Contents

Blame it on London

It's 5:30 in the morning and I am standing amidst the chaos of my newly decorated kitchen, eyeing the jumble of food and crockery scattered across the floor, considering all the suspects before me like Miss Marple. The fat one in the corner may have that 'Who me? I just got here' look on her face, but I'm not buying it. She's got plenty of form. The skinny one looks fairly innocent, until you notice that strand of last night's pasta hanging out the side of his mouth. He's chewing, slowly, hoping to get rid of the evidence without drawing any attention to himself. It's not working. Meanwhile, the enormous brown one with his back to me is studiously contemplating the cookbooks, apparently trying to decide if he's a Delia or a Jamie fan. Much of this stuff used to be up on the counter, far too high for his companions to have reached by themselves.

No one moves. They continue ignoring me, until the creaky grande dame, who sleeps outside my bedroom door, finally makes her way down the stairs and around the corner to join us. She shakes her head, gives me a 'Teenagers, what do you expect?' look, plops down, and nudges her bowl forward to remind me that it's never too early for breakfast. And so begins another bewildering day in the life of a Pet Nanny.

A Pet Nanny?

Yes, a nanny. For pets. Well, for dogs mostly. We're here when their owners can't be. Or, to be more accurate, they are here when their owners are elsewhere, usually somewhere either very sunny or very snowy. Why, you might ask, would someone who spent four years at university earning a degree in Anthropology, another two studying international relations at graduate school, and ten years building a promising career as an international diplomat, want to devote their life to caring for other people's dogs? This was certainly not what my career advisors had in mind.

I come from New York City – not Manhattan, of course, but fairly close to it. Growing up in such a multicultural place can make you go one of two ways: you either enjoy seeing hyphenated American life (as in Irish-American, Italian-American, Martian-American) or you want to go out and see the real thing. I enjoyed the St Patrick's Day parade down Fifth Avenue, in the days when they still painted the white line down the middle green, but I really wanted to know what the parade in Dublin would be like. Chinatown was great, but I suspected that Hong Kong was better. Michelangelo's *Pietà* looked beautiful at the Vatican Pavilion in the World's Fair, but how did it look in St

Peter's in Rome? You get the idea. As you can imagine, I was enormously difficult to live with.

Until, that is, Jimmy Carter decided that he really did need me in his diplomatic corps and so, after some training at the State Department and some liaising with the White House, much to my delight and everyone else's relief, I was off to explore the world. I became an American diplomat and served in Cameroon, Washington and Papua New Guinea. I trudged through the jungle with astronaut John Glenn and helped boxing legend Muhammad Ali in his search for warm water ports. I fled mutineering tuna fishermen in the South China Sea and snakes in an African shower, and I greeted American warships putting into harbour at dawn and missionary planes landing on rock-strewn fields at night. My diplomatic passport brought me respectful nods from customs agents and my security was assured day and night by the United States Marines.

Eventually I ended up in London. Disembarking at Heathrow during the dying days of the Reagan administration, I was headed for a wonderful two-year posting. A busy embassy in a major European capital perfectly balanced out my earlier posts in more remote regions. I was now perfectly positioned to clear the glass ceiling. My next station would be a senior job in some hot, humid, totally unpleasant little backwater that was hard to pronounce. My name might even end up on the door to the Ambassador's office.

I had high expectations for London, after a central casting stint in Washington. Just a few months earlier, I was tapped to work with the White House on special projects down the hall from the Oval Office. Suddenly I was dropping phrases like 'My counterpart at the White House and I think …' and 'I can't make the 2 o'clock meeting, I'll be over at the White House.'

Much as I had enjoyed opportunities to work in the White House, I was thrilled to have crossed the Atlantic. Who wouldn't want to be young and single and living in London, the home of Big Ben and the Beatles; red double-decker buses and black cabs; castles and cathedrals; fish and chips and country pubs; Wimbledon tennis and cricket.

I spent the next few months solving key problems, like helping a Florida high school marching band that had lost both their money and plane tickets find their way safely home. When senior citizens accidentally lost track of their tour groups, I was happy to help them reconnect. It was also my job to educate bewildered tourists on the meaning of 'tea time' and how it affected pub-opening hours. I loved them all; even the woman searching for a church her friend had recommended, the name and address of which she had forgotten, but it began with 'Saint'.

So, how exactly did I start off a lowly American diplomat and wind up an exalted English Pet Nanny? That's a very good question, one that I ask myself quite a lot. Sometimes I think about it when staring at the chewed edges of the antique silk rug that Great-Granddad brought back from China, or when looking for the frozen chicken that I was sure I had left defrosting in the kitchen, or when wondering if my brand new shoes are still wearable with only one heel. Or when shampooing the carpet, yet again.

Back then I had a great career, no student loans to pay off, a stable employer, no healthcare deductibles and a guaranteed civil service retirement plan. It never occurred to me that my wonderful position with the State Department was the second best job in town. Yet I jettisoned the lot after a chance meeting at a party with a charming journalist named Tom Arms.

I became determined to stay in London, a city we both adored, and I began to realise that there was more to life than the State Department. There were other things I wanted to do, like get married and have a family without having to raise children all over the world. And I wanted a dog.

The final step in my career transformation was brought about by my beloved husband Tom, who is the leader of our local Cub Scout pack. One evening he came home from knot-tying and fire-starting and said, 'I told Johnny that you would be a Pet Nanny. That's okay, isn't it?' Well, it's hard to listen too closely to anything a large, bald, one-eyed man in a giant Cub Scout uniform is saying but, and I say this from personal experience, that can be a mistake. It turns out that Tom's fellow Scouter is married to Serena, who runs a little business called, appropriately enough, Pet Nanny. She matches up people who need their furry friends cared for with people who would be happy to have a guest canine come and live in their home as part of the family. Being the persuasive sort of person she is, Serena has talked just about every dog lover even remotely connected with Scouting into becoming a Pet Nanny. The latest recruit, apparently, was me.

By not paying enough attention on that fateful evening and with absolutely no idea of what I was getting into or with any intention of getting into it, I woke up one morning to discover that a new chapter of my life was beginning. Not only that, but it suddenly seemed to be a role that I had been preparing for all my life: my previous canine encounters, my travels, my diplomatic background, all combined to give me the tools required to achieve success as a Pet Nanny. So the story really begins during my childhood, when my parents unknowingly set me on my destined path by bringing home my first ever dog – McTavish.

Astoria: The McTavish Years

My journey to Pet Nannyhood started a long, long time ago in a galaxy far, far away. Well, perhaps not that far away. Or, I suppose, even all that long ago, in the galactic scheme of things. But it was definitely on a very different planet, one called Astoria, in Queens, New York.

New York might have a reputation for being big and impersonal, but our little section of it was anything but. Everyone knew everyone else, either because they were from the same area 'back home' in the old country, or they went to the same school, or they lived in the same apartment building and sat out together on those green and white stripy garden chairs every summer night and watched the world go by. Or because they were related. For some reason, people in Astoria tended to have enormous extended families. I guess it's all those Irish Catholics marrying Italian Catholics. It must have made it easy to raise children, because everyone was always keeping an eye out for everyone else's child. It made it kind of hard to be the child though, since it was impossible to get away with anything. I had dozens of aunts and uncles and sixty-four first cousins, a depressingly large number of whom lived within watching distance of our front door. The memory of walking into the house after one particularly fun evening out and hearing my mother say, 'Yes, she's just coming in now', is still the stuff of nightmares.

I should probably confess right now that the entire goal of my young life was to get out of Astoria, New York. Looking back on it, I can't imagine why because it is actually a vibrant, colourful, fascinating place, in a weird sort of way. But at the time I just wanted to see more of the world. While everyone else worried about whether the Mets would ever win a World Series, I worried about whether I would ever see Gibraltar. Every Christmas I would ask if we could move to Montana. I have no idea why, other than that I couldn't think of a single city there.

For some reason, my parents' solution was to buy me a parakeet, named Billy.

Now, I had nothing against Billy, in fact I quite liked him, but he was really not enough to stop me from constantly leafing through copies of *National Geographic* and pointing out places where we could live instead. They must have noticed that most of the pictures I showed them involved children with dogs, because one night my father came home and, instead of hanging his jacket up in the closet as usual, he draped it over the knob of the door that I was sitting next to. Two seconds later, a head popped out of the pocket and stared at me. It was love at first sight, at least on my part.

McTavish (who we named after the robot in *Superman*, our favourite TV show) was a black, white and tan miniature toy fox terrier. Fully grown, he turned out to be less than a foot tall or long and weighed about the same as a medium-sized bag of potatoes. He was a great choice for a city apartment because miniature toy fox terriers apparently don't like the cold and prefer running around indoors. They are also very intelligent and have a great sense of humour. No, seriously. That's why they are used so often in clown acts. I am honestly not making this up. I would like to say that my father had put a lot of thought into this and decided that since we were an intelligent, funny, apartment-dwelling family, a miniature toy fox terrier would suit us perfectly, but I suspect that he just ran into someone in Conroy's, the bar down the road, who asked if he wanted a dog. Some things are just meant to be.

No one in my family had ever owned a dog before and so none of us realised that the entire house was not supposed to revolve around him. McTavish turned out to be a benevolent dictator who ruled his kingdom from the comfort of his box, which was kept right next to the radiator in the kitchen. It may have been a bit inconvenient for the rest of us but, as advertised, he just didn't like the cold. My mother, who was not a whimsical sort of person, used to dress him up in the most ridiculous outfits, allegedly to keep him from getting a chill. I still remember the time she cut four of the fingers off my father's leather gloves to make boots for the dog because it had started snowing. I have no idea what my father was supposed to do in arctic conditions without gloves but I guess she figured he didn't have to walk around in the snow on his hands. McTavish also had a plaid coat made, appropriately enough, out of McTavish tartan and a little beret with a pompom on it, but being a macho sort of a dog, that was going too far for him and he never actually wore that particular get-up.

My favourite outfit of his was the one that my mother had made up for my cousin Tommy's wedding. The bride's family decided that it was going to be a black tie affair, and all the men would wear tuxedos. This was just not an Astoria thing to do; tuxedos were generally limited to the ill-fitting kind normally worn by style-challenged teenagers to the prom. That wasn't, however, what they had in mind. They wanted the real thing. My mother, who was not one to take anything lying down, decided that if they wanted tuxedos, they were going to get tuxedos. She got a local seamstress to measure McTavish out for a dinner jacket, complete with frilled shirt, French cuffs, miniature cuff links, a little black bow tie and a hole in the back for his tail. When my cousin walked out of the church, the first thing he saw was McTavish, standing on his back legs, leaning against the wall, in all his glory. Tommy literally stopped in his tracks, threw back his head and started howling with laughter. Meanwhile, his wife of five minutes looked totally panic-stricken. I'm guessing she was wondering what she had just got herself into.

She wouldn't have been alone in that. We first met my future sister-in-law, Ann, when my brother Dennis brought her home for one of McTavish's birthday parties. She still talks about the experience of walking in to find us all sat around the table wearing party hats. After dinner we sang 'Happy Birthday' as my mother carried in the cake from the special bakery we used for all of our big-occasion cakes. It had white icing with 'Happy Birthday McTavish' written in blue piping (because he was a boy) and was decorated all around the edges with miniature bones. McTavish needed help blowing out the candles but he could open the presents all by himself. Ann said she spent the entire evening wondering if we were kidding, while making sure that she never let any of us get between her and the door, just in case we weren't. Of course, she now has a dog named Presley who has an Elvis outfit, complete with cape and sunglasses, which she dresses him up in every Halloween. Dennis must have known she had it in her.

I absolutely loved McTavish, but my brother Jimmy wasn't so sure about him. For one thing, McTavish would bark whenever anyone came in the front door, which was a problem for Jimmy as he used to frequently try to sneak in hours after he was supposed to be home from some big date or other. He developed a system that involved flinging open the door as quickly as he could, thus trying to catch McTavish off guard, while throwing down a fistful of dog biscuits and then rushing in to get undressed and into bed before McTavish had time to finish them. I have to say that despite the fact that he is six feet and five inches tall, my brother could certainly move fast when he wanted to, so my mother was always wondering why the dog would suddenly start barking in the middle of the night when we were all fast asleep in bed. I have no idea what his various girlfriends thought about the fact that he used to show up on dates with his pockets full of dog biscuits, but he probably came up with some convincing story. He did, after all, grow up to be a lawyer.

Jimmy's height was another problem for him, at least as far as walking the dog went. It couldn't have been easy being young, distinctly tall, living in a neighbourhood where everyone knew you and having to walk a dog that weighed six pounds and was less than a foot high. Especially a dog with a Napoleonic complex, who took it as a challenge to make sure that, despite his size, everyone knew he was there by growling menacingly, or at least as menacingly as a dog his size could achieve. Jimmy's solution was to put McTavish under his coat, walk the few blocks to where we kept the car, drive to another neighbourhood and walk him there.

My father, meanwhile, thought that McTavish was the most intelligent dog in the world, not that he really knew all that many other dogs. This conclusion was based entirely on the fact that McTavish always barked when anyone left the house, except on Sunday mornings when we were going out to church. Dad was convinced that McTavish knew it was a Sunday because Jackie Gleason's popular Saturday night show had been on the night before.

He never explained why it was only outings to church that caused McTavish's silence, rather than those to work or school. Or for that matter why he didn't bark on those rare Sundays when we hadn't watched Jackie Gleason the night before. Personally, I was convinced that the reason lay more in his efforts to digest all those biscuits my brother had given him a few hours earlier, than in his religious leanings or television viewing preferences.

McTavish really was a great dog. He didn't cure me of my desire to get out of Astoria but he certainly played a big part in my many happy memories of it, and of my childhood. He also turned us into a family of dog lovers. In fact, since McTavish's day, we have never spent even an hour without at least one dog somewhere in the family. All of them have been wonderful characters in their own rights, but McTavish was special. He was the first.

Washington: The Aristide Years

I did eventually leave Astoria by taking the unusual, although not completely unheard of, step of going away to college. But McTavish came with me, at least in spirit. My family put him on the line every time I called home, and he sent me lots of cards, all of which he signed himself. It involved paws and ketchup, in case you're wondering. Somehow, knowing that he, and my parents, were still at home and waiting for me to come back, made it possible to leave. Not that I went all that far, at least not at first – just to upstate New York.

Being at university in Binghamton, New York, was exciting at first – a place where grass did not grow in perfect rectangles and trees did not have fences around them. But it soon became apparent that it really wasn't much of a change – everyone still looked, sounded and thought just like, and in fact, were, New Yorkers. The few people who did not come from within twenty miles of New York City tended to either stick together or else keep their heads down and hope they didn't get mugged by the rest of us.

One day, near the end of my sophomore year, I picked up a leaflet in the Student Union for a meeting of the International Studies Association, and since it was just about to start and I had nothing else to do, I wandered over. It turned out that the university had set up a programme where you could study abroad for your third year. They would send you somewhere foreign (the where depending on what you were studying) as a small group, complete with a professor. The only qualification you needed to get on the programme was a willingness to go.

In fact, they were so grateful if you signed up that they sent a thank you note. They had me, as the saying goes, at hello. Of course, since there was only a handful of students and just the one professor willing to give it a try, the choice of destinations wasn't endless. In fact, it was Malta. But that suited me just fine.

Malta was everything I was hoping 'abroad' would be. Right in the middle of the Mediterranean, it was filled with sights and sounds and colours that had nothing to do with Astoria, and with people who not only weren't, but who didn't want to be, Americans. At the time I was studying Archaeology, but my desire to be an archaeologist lasted about two weeks, if that. Once you have stood beside a prehistoric burial site in the hot Mediterranean sun and tried to figure out whether something was a goat bone or a sheep bone, you have pretty much done it, in my opinion. And by then I was already much more inter- ested in the political rally that was going on just down the hill. That was filled with real, live people, shouting in some strange, vaguely Italian, vaguely Arabic language, waving banners and getting extremely worked up about something. I still don't know what. But I threw myself so into it all that by the end of the year I had mastered at least five sentences in Maltese, some of which were even suitable for repeating to my parents' friends back home, changed my major to Anthropology and decided that I was going to spend a great deal more time in the wonder- ful world of 'abroad'.

Sadly, first I had to go back to Binghamton for another whole year, to finish up my degree. It's not easy to go backwards once you have found what you want. Suffice it to say that for the entire year I never left my room without taking my passport with me, just in case. I'm still not sure in case of what. As this was Binghamton, hometown of *The Twilight Zone*'s Rod Serling, I was more likely to be abducted by aliens, in which case I probably wouldn't have needed my passport, than to be offered a foreign trip at any point between breakfast and dinner.

My parents really have my brother to blame for what came next. Jimmy couldn't decide whether he wanted to be a lawyer or a diplomat, until he realised that trial lawyers were guaranteed bigger audiences on a more regular basis than diplomats. And so, once he had also realised that I had been bitten by the travel bug, he started sending me 'Be a diplomat' messages. In one of them, he enclosed the prospectus for the Georgetown University School of Foreign Service's graduate programme. As no airline wanted me as a stewardess and since I couldn't think of anything else to do, I applied.

After a few nail-biting months, a thick envelope dropped through the letterbox. Those are always the best kind to get when you are waiting to hear the results of an application, but I was still nervous about opening it. You never know, those Washington types might have had an evil sense of humour. But, thankfully, they didn't. Georgetown wanted me and I was off to Washington as fast as Amtrak could carry me. Soon I was meeting people who also never left home without their passports. It was wonderful to be with people who all dreamed of the same thing: to live and work abroad.

Meanwhile, several of my friends from Malta, via Binghamton, had also decided to move to Washington. Steve was already at law school there, while Karen and Robin decided that they might as well work in Washington as anywhere else, so we set up house together on Capitol Hill. Well, near Capitol Hill – the dodgy end. We had a great time recreating our glory days in Malta, although we had to learn to tone it down a bit when we realised that our new friends were all rolling their eyes every time a sentence started 'When we were in Malta …'

We weren't there long before we decided that, now that we were grown-ups with a flat of our own, we needed a dog. Well, to be perfectly honest, three of us decided that. Steve was far too busy trying to make law review to be worrying about the fact that our house was not a home. So, without ever really discussing this with him, and I have to say that I belatedly do feel badly about that, we three girls went down to the local pound and came back with the world's ugliest dog.

It's hard to describe him. Try to picture what Central Casting would send over if the call went out for a medium-sized, shaggy yet slightly scrawny, indeterminate-coloured beast with really kind eyes and a perpetual shiver. I loved him, but he really was odd-looking. So odd-looking, in fact, that you had no choice but to love him. He was the Barbra Streisand of the canine world, so ugly that he was beautiful, at least to us. Aristide, named after Monsieur Briand, the man in the poster that was hanging in every college dorm room in the world at the time, was no longer *dans son cabaret* and was, instead, soon in our living room. Steve was totally appalled when he came home from classes one day and discovered a dog of no discernible breeding lying on the sofa. He immediately announced that he was having absolutely nothing to do with the creature, and stayed true to his word – I have absolutely no other memories that include the both of them.

Now, I have to say that we didn't really think this plan through. First, we were all either out at school or work all day, so walking the dog was a bit of a problem. Then there was the fact that Aristide was completely crazy. There's no other word for it. He would spend his days lying on his back, in the middle of the sofa, staring at the ceiling. No amount of throwing balls around the sitting room would help. Scratching his tummy was fine, he didn't mind if we did it, as long as we didn't interrupt his view. He particularly liked one corner of the ceiling and would watch that spot for hours at a time. Eventually no one would sit underneath it. We all knew it probably wasn't haunted, or anything like that, but it didn't hurt to be on the safe side.

Besides the ceiling, Aristide's other great love was food, although here too he had a particular quirk. It had to be food that you had poured an enormous amount of oil over. We discovered this when, after several weeks of worrying about the fact that the dog wasn't eating, Karen accidentally knocked over a bottle of vegetable oil and some of it fell into Aristide's dish. He was on it like a shot. Robin, who was walking into the kitchen at that moment, was nearly bowled over. Aristide never looked back after that. He would eat anything, as long as it was swimming in oil. I'm not sure what it did for his arteries, but he did have an amazingly shiny coat.

While Aristide may have been a bit quirkier than we had bargained for, he really did make us into a family, or three-quarters of us at least. His presence had the unexpected result of making us part of the neighbourhood, in a way that as mere students we never would have been, as we soon came to know all our fellow dog-walking neighbours. Aristide also helped improve relations with our landlord, who lived downstairs from us. He was not the world's most friendly individual, until we asked him if Aristide could spend some time in his back-yard if the weather was nice. One thing led to another, and before we knew it Aristide was spending his days downstairs and his nights upstairs. It never ceases to amaze me how a dog can make your life better in so many ways.

While my domestic life might have been something approaching bliss, I had to decide what to do about my pro-fessional one. Diplomat or banker? Banker or diplomat? In the end I decided that being a diplomat just had to be more fun than being a banker (for some reason I never considered the idea of doing a job just to make money) and so I set my sights on the State Department. The day I was sworn in as a Foreign Service Officer was sunny and wonderful. And after a few exciting years of addressing UN meetings, working at the African Bureau, and finding excuses to walk past the Oval Office when it really wasn't on the way to anywhere I had to go, I finally received my first overseas posting. I was heading off to be a junior diplomat in Papua New Guinea and so I had to say goodbye to everyone, including Aristide.

He wouldn't have fitted into my luggage allowance, even if I could have convinced Robin and Karen to let me take him, but the question of what to do with him had started to become rather pressing. Robin had decided to become a teacher and was heading back to New York for her training. Karen was going to move into a studio, where a dog would not be happy. Steve was still pretending that the dog didn't exist, and to our total astonishment and disbelief, our landlord had actually got married and had a baby and was not really in the market for a full-time dog. So Aristide found a new home with Robin's parents and younger sisters. It made sense. Robin was the only one with a car, and so had taken the dog home with her every holiday. Her sisters, who were desperate for a pet, had fallen so in love with him that they were constantly sending him little cards and notes in the post. And her parents, well they just gave up and gave in. Aristide became a New Yorker and spent the rest of his life being fussed over by two pretty little blonde girls, while staring with total concentration at a new ceiling.

PNG: The Puppy Years

There were twenty-five of us due to receive our assignments on the same day at the State Department, and a list of openings that included Paris, Munich, Rome, Tokyo, Buenos Aires and Montreal. Strangely enough, everyone was very excited about those. I, on the other hand, couldn't believe my luck – Papua New Guinea was also on the list. I had a degree in Anthropology and my heroine, Margaret Mead, had done most of her work there. How could I possibly give up the chance of following in her footsteps? My hand was up and waving in a shot. Twenty-four people stared at me in complete and utter disbelief, and in sheer relief. I don't think I've ever been as popular in my life as I was that day. And so, a few weeks later, in February, I was off to the airport, driving through snow that came up past your waist. My parents spent the entire trip arguing about who was to blame for this.

It's hard to know what to say about Papua New Guinea, or PNG as we locals called it. It was, quite simply, the absolute end of the universe. In fact, even now, all these years later, it is still one of the least explored places on earth and many undiscovered plants, animals and, for all I know, people are still out there, not waiting to be found.

One of the first things I noticed about Papua New Guinea, other than how insanely hot and humid it was, was that everyone seemed to be speaking a different language. I wasn't just imagining it. Out of a then population of about three million people, PNG had over 850 different languages – completely different mind you, not just dialects. This is mainly because the country is just so hard to get around. In terms of environments, you name it, PNG has it, from dense tropical rainforests to rugged mountains to large wetlands. People could live five miles apart but be so divided by geography that they never met, and so they developed not only mutually incomprehensible languages but also completely separate cultures, customs, costumes, music, art, everything. It was like being back at the UN, except hotter, harder to get to and, well, weirder.

I was the youngest member of staff at the embassy, which meant that I got all the jobs that no one else really wanted, including Youth Liaison Officer, which mostly involved mingling and drinking with the university students, and acting Military Attaché. The latter kept me busy as Washington was always including us in directives that they sent to all the major Pacific countries, and so I would be instructed to approach the PNG army for this and the air force for that. One time they wanted me to ask the navy if it would be interested in joint naval manoeuvres. I sent a message back saying they would but their boat was being painted. Strangely enough, no one but me thought that was funny.

After being in PNG for a while, you learned to take most things in your stride. After all, this was a place where you could turn around in a shop and encounter a man with a hole in his nose through which you could see the shelf beside him. At which point you would spot a particular item on that shelf and your only thought would be, 'Oh, I forgot salt.' It took a lot to get you really excited – like the arrival of an astronaut.

John Glenn was the first person to orbit the earth. He was also an ex-Marine, a US Senator and an extremely nice man. He came out to Papua New Guinea on his way to the Solomon Islands independence ceremonies. We put a lot of thought into where to take Senator Glenn while he was visiting us. He was, after all, a very adventurous man. Luckily, we knew some American missionaries who worked in a remote village and we were sure they would be happy to show a former astronaut just what traditional life was like on PNG. And so, we headed off, first by plane then on foot, into the interior.

Glenn's visit had many memorable moments, but one of my favourites was when the missionaries told the villagers about his trip into space. Either they didn't know the real story or the message got lost in translation, but the villagers thought that he had actually been on the moon and not just near it. This was an important distinction, as it turned out, because in their religion when a man dies his soul goes to the moon. And so, here in front of them was a man who must have died and returned to life. It would be hard to overstate the reverence with which they treated him after that.

The children, however, were less awestruck and asked him a million questions. One of them was 'How fast did your space-ship go?' He told them some speed in miles per second that didn't mean a thing to them, and so he asked how long it was to Kokoda, the nearest town. It was twenty-five miles away. How long would it take to walk there? Three days. And so he took out his watch and said, 'When I snap my fingers, I am over your village in my spaceship. When I snap them again, I am over Kokoda.' He looked at his watch, snapped his fingers once and almost immediately snapped them again. For a second no one made a sound and then everyone in the village, men, women, children, even dogs I think, started cheering and clapping and trying to touch his sleeve. It was a remarkable experience, for all of us.

But I bet you are really wondering how any of this helped me on my journey to Pet Nannyhood. Well, being in Papua New Guinea taught me a very valuable lesson: how to share a dog. I'm almost certain that Puppy *was* a dog, although I honestly couldn't begin to tell you what breed(s). He was waist-high and slightly built, with black fur, four legs and a tail. That's the best I can do, really. I suppose there were little bits of every kind of dog the expat community had been bringing to PNG for the last fifty years, along with a few local components. No one really knew. Neither did anyone know where he came from nor what his name was, he just turned up outside my front door one day. My neighbour, Geoff, and I asked around for a bit and then we just adopted him. We called him Puppy, not only because he had that ungainly, not fully formed look about him, but also because Geoff point-blank refused to call him Pumpkin and I refused to call him Cedric.

Puppy became part of our lives and would sleep outside under a little roof that was between our two front doors, on a bed we had made for him. Geoff got up earlier than I did and so would give him his breakfast and play with him on the beach for a while before going off to work. Puppy would then spend the day roaming the neighbourhood but would be waiting for me for his dinner and some serious ball-tossing when I got home from work. Neither one of us knew what Puppy got up to when we weren't around, but he seemed to be not only thriving but actually putting on a little bit of weight. This went on for months, with Geoff, Puppy and me all very happy with the arrangement.

Until Puppy's owner turned up one day and demanded to know why we were feeding his dog. It turned out that Puppy didn't actually sleep outside on the bed we had so lovingly made for him, he just turned up early enough for his breakfast and made sure he was back in time for his dinner. He apparently had this arrangement with quite a few other people and so spent most of his time walking from one bowl to another. I have to admit that I was rather surprised by this turn of events but it did explain why the dog was beginning to resemble one of PNG's world-famous pigs. Geoff and I apologised to the owner for loving his dog, which seemed to take him slightly aback, and promised not to feed him any more. We dismantled his bed that evening and felt a real sense of loss as we said good-night to each other. We didn't need to worry, though, because the next morning Puppy was back. He didn't get breakfast but he did get his morning walk along the beach, and was back in the evening for playtime with his ball. We kept our word about the food, except for the odd treat of course, and Puppy gradually lost some weight. We never found out what his name was though. We never asked. No matter what his owner called him, he was Puppy to us.

London: A New Start

I can't honestly say that I was sorry to leave Papua New Guinea, although I knew that I would be telling PNG stories for the rest of my life. It was absolutely the strangest place I had ever been to, but now I was ready for a big city and a return to normalcy.

I can't remember the exact date that I arrived in London, but it was a sunny day in September. That narrows it down considerably. I was picked up at the airport by someone who obviously had better things to do, because he barely had time to open the door, throw my bags in the hall and tell me not to mind the Marines before he rushed off, missing my response of 'What?' Apparently, I was being placed in temporary housing as my real accommodation was being refurbished or repainted or something else that started with re, but in the meantime I could stay here, on a busy road, in a one bedroom flat, next door to a Marine House containing a score of twenty-something year-olds with buzz cuts. I quickly figured out that the reason the plaster was coming away from the walls was due to a combination of the ear-splitting music coming through them and the overpowering sound of buses and trucks changing gears on the hill a foot or two outside them. Or perhaps it was just the way English flats were constructed.

I decided to go out and explore my new city. I wandered around for hours and saw the Thames and Trafalgar Square, walked around Hyde Park and over to Buckingham Palace, then strolled down Regent Street and on to the Houses of Parliament. While it was all very exciting at first, I soon came to realise that being a newcomer in a big city where you don't know anyone is a pretty lonely place to be. I decided to go back and see what the Marines were up to – not a happy prospect.

I was waiting for a bus near Big Ben and probably looking very sorry for myself. I didn't know anyone, I was far from home, I was going to be here for years whether I liked it or not. The man next to me in the queue asked if I was all right and when the bus came, we got on, sat together and started talking about our situations. He had been at the Ministry of Defence for thirty-five years but he was retiring on the coming Friday. He was looking forward to spending time with his grandchildren and pottering in his garden, but he couldn't believe how quickly the years had gone. I told him I was here all alone and envied him his family and garden. He told me not to worry and that he had a feeling that everything was going to work out just fine, and then he got off the bus. I hated seeing him go, he was my best friend in the whole country. As the bus pulled out, he stood on the pavement, smiled and tipped his hat at me. I felt instantly better and began to believe that perhaps it would be all right after all. I have often thought about him and wished I could tell him that he was right, and that it did.

In the end, it didn't take too long for me to find my feet. And then I met Tom and the rest is history. Some things, I suppose, are meant to be. I wasn't planning on staying at the party where we met; I was going to just drop in for a minute on the way to another one. He had only met the woman holding it the day before and came on a whim. But we were both there and have been together ever since.

I guess this is as good a time as any to introduce you to the other humans in my household so that you don't get confused trying to work out who has a tail and who doesn't. My boy Christopher is the next generation of dog lover, as long as the dog does not wander into his room. He is the chief ball-thrower and dog-walking assistant, tug-of-war player and lifter of heavy dogs. His older sister Kimberly is the cuckoo in our nest. She just does not like dogs. I have absolutely no idea how that happened. She has been around them since, literally, the day she was born. Perhaps that explains it. Or perhaps it's because she doesn't think it's funny when she comes home and finds a large dog sleeping in her bed, with the remains of her favourite belt still hanging out of his mouth. Whatever the reason for her bizarre feelings, I have faith that she will one day be able to put them aside, learn to share her home with this motley assortment of creatures and, dare I say it, even start to enjoy it a bit.

But before my children could arrive on the scene, I first had to contend with the upheaval that my decision to stay in London would bring. It meant leaving the State Department, which wasn't easy to start with, and I then needed to think of something else that I was meant to do. My next step was to become a journalist, which was a profession I enjoyed but, even so, I suspected that something was missing. I just didn't know what.

To be honest, I didn't think about it all that much. I was too busy. As the years passed and the children came, so did their schools, friends and hobbies, which involved a lot of time sitting on insanely uncomfortable benches watching Kimberly in plays, and standing on wind-swept fields watching Christopher play rugby. Between work, friends, children and relatives we had our hands full. But as our lives moved forwards, things continued to change. The children not only grew, they grew up, and gradually I realised that there was now room for something else.

But what? I was good at crowd control, dealing with sibling squabbles, lateral thinking, juggling schedules, being fond of small creatures who were not necessarily my own, handling challenges and meeting new people. I loved dogs and lived in a country that was mad about them, near a common and in a neighbourhood that had almost as many dogs in it as it did people.

This might explain one of the first things you notice when you move to London, other than the weather of course, which is the huge number of green spaces, dotted around one of the most crowded cities in the world. In New York, there's one big patch of grass in the centre, and concrete everywhere else. In other American towns, there are a lot of sizeable yards. Not here. In Britain, the houses are packed together with pocket handkerchief gardens, where they exist at all. To compensate, however, there is usually a large, open space no more than 100 yards from most people's front door. This is because London, like the rest of Britain, wasn't planned or laid out to a grid like urban America. It simply evolved, over thousands of years. London itself started off as a Roman-built square mile (now the financial district) and then over the centuries it expanded, swallowing up all the surrounding villages in the process. Each of those villages had commons protected by common law and so they remain to this day.

All of this, besides being an interesting little historical titbit, makes London a paradise for British dogs and their owners. The dogs have somewhere to walk, run and explore, and plenty of trees to piddle against, hide behind, eat fruit from, and chase squirrels up. But these commons aren't just dog havens, they are also the focal point of a lot of other activities. So you'll find exercise groups running around in circles, and kite-flyers running up and down in straight lines, and children running every which way. There are picnickers and footballers and even occasional sunbathers, all of whom are potential playmates for the dogs, whether they want to be or not. Which could explain the shouts of 'Drop that' or 'Come back with that' or the ever-useful 'Nooooooo!' that are all frequently to be heard on most British commons.

Our local green haven, and the geographical centre of our universe, is Wandsworth Common, which suffers from an identity crisis. Nestled between the prison at one end and a mental hospital at the other, it thinks it's in the country, despite being crossed by a rather busy road.

Perhaps it thinks this because a large section of it has been left to nature. Trees, especially horse chestnuts, soar overhead. Bushes filled with berries are scattered all around. Earth is beaten down to form paths through the undergrowth. Once a year or so, the council sends round people to trim the trees and thin out the undergrowth and it always comes as a rather nasty surprise that you can suddenly see flashes of cars as they whiz by or, more likely, as they stand absolutely motionless in yet another epic traffic jam.

The rest of the Common is a bit more manicured, but lovely nonetheless. There is an enormous pond with a pretty stone bridge over it, wooden walkways around it and lots of ducks, geese and fishermen in it. I can't honestly say if there are any fish in it as well. I've never seen any, and I suspect that the fishermen haven't either. Still, that doesn't seem to bother them. There is a second, much smaller, pond that has a little water feature in it like you see in rather swish aquariums, the kind that half-heartedly throws a bit of water into the air in the hope that it some of it will get oxygenated. I'm guessing that it's not working all that well, because I can't remember the last time there wasn't a sign there warning me not to let my dog (or child, I suppose) swim in it because of the 'algae situation'. There's another bridge, which in an ideal world would be over a sparkling stream but, this being London, actually crosses the railway tracks. What it lacks in rural charm, though, it more than makes up for in importance as the centre of the Common. You only have to stand there for a few seconds before you start meeting walkers, joggers, bikers, babies in prams and, of course, dogs. Millions of dogs.

Being a Pet Nanny means you get to spend a lot of time up on the Common. But, then again, being almost anything in this neighbourhood means you are fairly likely to find yourself up there quite a lot of the time. Everyone uses the Common, for an amazing variety of things. Early in the morning and around late afternoon, it is filled with children going to and from school. There are a lot of schools here, and a lot of children. In fact, there are statistically more children here per square inch than anywhere else on the planet except, perhaps, Mumbai. I heard that somewhere. Probably up on the Common.

To be a child in this neighbourhood, you have to pass some stringent tests. First of all, you have to have a name like Arabella, Araminta, Ollie or Freddie. With children named Kimberly and Christopher I obviously didn't spot this in time. It's okay, though, my two have learned to respond to Arabella and Ollie whenever necessary. Children also need to have the fortitude to go to school in – let's be kind – 'unusual' clothes: pinafores and straw boaters for the girls, while the boys wear those trousers that come just below the knee. But the most important skill is the ability to not listen to a word your mother is saying. As in, 'Araminta, darling, please stop trying to throw your brother into the pond.' To be followed by, 'Araminta, please don't do it again, darling' and finally, 'Minty, Mummy is getting very upset.'

The dogs, by contrast, are a fairly well-behaved bunch. That's because most of them have been to residential obedience schools somewhere out in the country, or else have had so many lessons with the pet psychologist that they have decided that it's easier to stay out of the pond than it is to listen yet again to someone with a soft voice and a bean bag telling them to stop and think about what they are doing before they do it.

I have no idea what the point of the bean bag is but it seems to work, unless a picnic is involved. Let's face it, if the choice is between a bean bag and a smoked salmon sandwich, very few dogs are going to go for the beans. Especially if being told not to by someone in a very soft voice.

But with only a very few exceptions, the dogs are welcomed – even loved – by the British public at large. In fact, dog ownership is one of the great breakers of the famous British reserve. Take a dog for a walk and within minutes a complete stranger will be walking up to the dog, bending over, scratching it behind the ears and asking the dog, 'And what's your name?' Of course, they can't actually ask the owner. No, British social mores dictate that you don't talk to strangers until you have been properly introduced. The dog is the introduction. You answer for the dog and before long you and a complete stranger have moved on to discussing the dog's breed and age, then the weather, children … and you're off. Ownership of a dog is a particularly good way for a foreigner to meet the natives. Once the locals have detected a foreign accent, the reserve disappears and is replaced by a bottomless curiosity: why you are in Britain? What brought you to the country? What do you think of the weather? What part of America do you come from?

In fact, dog ownership is such an effective ice-breaker that a friend of mine once toyed with the idea of setting up a business based upon it. She was going to rent out dogs to foreigners who wanted to meet British people. She wasn't certain whether to hand the dogs out at Heathrow or to open a rent-a-dog concession at Hyde Park but she knew that wherever she put it, it would make a fortune. Of course, she wasn't British and, after seeing the horrified looks on people's faces when she told them about it, she also insisted that she wasn't serious. Just as well. For one thing, the Royal Society for the Prevention of Cruelty to Animals would have got wind of the scheme and they would not have been happy.

And speaking of the RSPCA, only in Britain would you have a ROYAL Society for the Prevention of Cruelty to Animals, complete with royal patronage and all its trappings, when the Society for the Prevention of Cruelty to Children is a mere NATIONAL (NSPCC). That alone tells you all you need to know about the British attitude towards their pets – an attitude I was soon to adopt with the arrival of my first London dog, Scrumpy; a dog who was very definitely not meant for London.

Scrumpy

The title of oddest dog I ever encountered almost certainly goes to Scrumpy the Border collie. I can't blame Scrumpy on anyone, other than Tom of course, because she was mine. She was Tom's thirtieth-birthday present to me. We had just got married and I was settling into south London but missing my family, and he thought that a dog would be just the thing I needed. It was a good plan but unfortunately, and this is a trait that I have become exceedingly familiar with over the years, he didn't really think it through.

The big day arrived and so did Scrumpy, a black and white fur ball with an enormous personality. And lots of energy. Apparently that shouldn't have been too surprising since Border collies are very intelligent, very hard-working dogs who excel in any activities that require agility skills. As you may know, they are particularly good at sheep-herding and Ultimate Frisbee-catching. Farmers, and I suppose Ultimate Frisbee players, love them because they have enormous stamina levels. They are also good-natured and loyal.

I guess when Tom was researching what kind of dog he should get and read the Border collie entry in *What Dog to Buy for a Small Flat in a Big City*, he just skipped down to that last part and thought, 'Since we live in a third-floor flat and both work all day, a good-natured and loyal dog will be perfect.' What other explanation could there be?

I had no idea what a sheepdog was, but I soon got the idea. Scrumpy took one look around her new home and noted the glaring absence of sheep. But she didn't let that bother her. She decided to herd me and Tom instead. Scrumpy literally could not bear it if we were in separate rooms. She would slink down and get to work, making a large figure of eight, where I was in one circle and Tom in the other. Gradually she would make the figure smaller, pushing each of us a little closer to the middle until we were at least in positions where she could lie down and keep us both in sight. It made life a little difficult when one of us was cooking while the other tried to have a bath, but she had more energy than we did and could keep at it longer, so we learned to adapt.

There was one situation, however, in which she just couldn't win. Tom used to be a regular guest on a London talk radio station and so he would happily go off to the studio while Scrumpy and I stayed at home to be the audience. Well, to be perfectly honest, Scrumpy was the audience. I was busy trying to save the stereo. The speakers were too large to go on top of anything, so we had them on the floor, on either side of the sofa. Usually Scrumpy ignored them, but whenever Tom was on she went into action. The only problem was that he appeared to be on both sides of the room at the same time, and no amount of circling got one of him closer to the other. When herding didn't work, she started nipping at where she guessed the speakers' heels were. Sadly, that didn't work either. She may have had an abundance of energy, but even she got tired eventually. That's when she ate them. Not all of them, of course – just the parts where the sound came from. I suppose it solved the problem in a way.

There were many sounds that Scrumpy didn't like, but she had a particular aversion to Tom's rendition of 'Happy Birthday'. Now, if you had ever heard Tom sing, you would probably have some sympathy with her, but she didn't seem to mind the rest of his repertoire. She just hated 'Happy Birthday'. As soon as he started, she would howl. If that didn't work, she would start leaping up and down in the air. If he kept going, she would launch herself at him like a missile. Luckily it's a short song so she only had to use the last resort a few times, which was to bite him on the bottom. That was pretty impressive when I come to think about it, considering how tall he is and how small she was. Tom's lack of ingenuity was also fairly impressive – he never thought to shut Scrumpy in another room when the cake was due to come out. I have to say, I did, but I couldn't bring myself to mention it. It was just too entertaining to watch.

Scrumpy had lots of other great tricks. She always sat in a particular chair so she could look out the window and keep tabs on the neighbourhood. Guests, of course, generally didn't know that it was her chair. If she came into the room and found it occupied, she would back up to the door in order to get some momentum, start running towards the chair and then leap, smacking whoever was in it in the chest before landing in their lap and circling around to lie down. Tom's friend Rory had the misfortune of having just been handed a large glass of whisky, which he had really been looking forward to, right before Scrumpy came round the corner. It took ages to get that stain off the ceiling.

You may be wondering why we never mentioned this little quirk to guests before they sat down. I honestly don't know the answer to that, but I suspect it was because Scrumpy was my first-born and everything she did was okay with me. And it provided a continuing source of amusement.

Sadly our happy state didn't last for ever because three years later my real first-born arrived, Kimberly. The two of them didn't take to each other, each believing they came first in the pecking order. Scrumpy was fine as long as the baby didn't move, but once she started crawling things got a bit out of hand. The basic problem was that Kimberly just didn't get the whole herding concept and figure-of-eight pattern, or the need to avoid various spots on the floor from which Scrumpy would launch herself, either into her chair, or towards the light fixture in a never-ending attempt to capture a fly that had been there years earlier. Kimberly wanted to go where she wanted to go, whether the dog liked it or not. It reached a head one evening: Kimberly crawled under the dining room table when Scrumpy happened to be there already. Scrumpy wasn't in the mood to play and as I raced over to grab the baby, she turned around and started growling.

As luck would have it there was, at that very moment, a pet psychologist doing a phone-in show on the radio. Tom called up, was put through and recounted what had just happened. The psychologist said to him, 'Why on earth are you calling me when you should be calling someone to come and get the dog?', or words to that effect. He had a point. A few days later, we waved goodbye, as Scrumpy set off to a new life, herding sheep on a farm in Wales. You just know she was happier there than she ever was with us. It's where she should have been all along.

Not that I would ever admit that to Kimberly. All these years later and whenever she annoys me, which is frequently, I still tell her that I gave up my dog for her and that I'm not sure I made the right decision. Which is true – at least half of it anyway.

Looking back on it now, I realise that we could, perhaps, have done a few things better as far as Scrumpy was concerned. For a start, we could have had a completely different dog, one who was more suitable to our lifestyle and housing arrangements. And then it probably would have helped if we had trained her just a little. At least enough so that the entire household didn't revolve around her, so that guests could sit, or sing, wherever and whatever they wanted while visiting us. But I loved her, warts and all. It's as simple as that.

Having Scrumpy in my life made me happy. And memories of her still do, thinking back on her. Letting her go was hard, but not as hard as I thought it would be. For one thing, I knew that I had no choice, Kimberly's safety obviously came first. For another, I knew she really was going to a better place. But even while waving her off to Wales, I knew that we needed a dog in our lives. It just wasn't the right time.

My life with Scrumpy made me realise something else – pet owners can be totally crazy when it comes to their pets. I know, because I was. So it's something I can fully appreciate, and treasure, in my Pet Nanny clients. If Angus needs forty toys to make his overnight stay happy, who am I to say it isn't so, despite the fact that he never once looks at any of them. If Alfie gets an email every night which his family want me to read out to him, I'm happy to do it. When someone arrives with their greyhound/lurcher who needs hours and hours of exercise a day or else he starts chewing on the furniture, well, I can't honestly say that I don't understand how it happened.

If truth be told, I love crazy owners. Not only are they immensely entertaining, but they're my kind of people.

Gaby

We didn't have a dog for a long time after Scrumpy. Kimberly was joined a few years later by her brother Christopher and life was taken up with all the things that make up the routine of a family with growing children. Nurseries gave way to schools, sand pits turned into rugby pitches, play dates became sleepovers. Life moved on. But our dog-free existence was never destined to last.

I blame Christopher. He wanted a dog. I wasn't sure. I already had a husband, two children, a job and a house, not to mention tons of potted plants and some goldfish. Did I really need a dog? No, I did not. I kept hoping that he would forget all about it but as his birthday approached, he stepped up the pressure. He was pushing against an open door as far as Tom was concerned. He thought it would be a good idea for Christopher to take on some responsibility and that having a dog would be just the thing. What?! Was he really telling me that he was the one parent on the planet who actually believed the words 'I'll take care of the dog and walk it and feed it and everything'? He claimed he was, despite the fact that he had once been a boy with a dog himself. But I wasn't fooled. He wanted a dog and he was using our son to get one.

I told my mother, knowing that she would be on my side, but she just laughed and said that I wasn't kidding anyone by pretending that I didn't want a dog. The more I denied it, the more she laughed. It was very annoying, especially since it wasn't true. At that point, I did not feel as if I had a dog-sized hole in my life, but it was fast becoming apparent that other people did, and they were getting vocal.

I cracked, a bit. I started saying 'if' instead of 'no'. It was all they needed. The runaway train started gathering momentum. When they began talking about Irish wolfhounds and Siberian huskies, I knew that I had to wrest back control and inject some sanity into the proceedings. So I went up to the Common and did my research. I approached every dog owner I saw (well, every owner of a dog that I would even remotely consider having) and asked them about their dog and about how good it was with children. It was a waste of time really because every single one was, apparently, absolutely lovely and completely wonderful with children. I had my doubts about one or two of them, but I have to admit that most really did look like great dogs. Then I noticed that I had gradually started speaking to people with cocker spaniels more often than to people with any other kind of breed. The blue roans, in particular, were beautiful dogs and seemed genuinely good-natured. Plus, it must be said, there were an awful lot of them up there. It's that kind of neighbourhood.

By this time, I had given up on the 'if' and my family had started working on the 'when', so I put in some stipulations which I was certain would slow down the inevitable. It had to be a girl because they were nicer than boys. That was okay with Christopher. It had to be a cocker spaniel. Agreed. We had just had the sitting room done up so it couldn't be a puppy. I wanted an older, already housetrained dog. I thought I had him there, but he didn't mind. Perhaps he really did want a dog after all.

I spent the next several weeks trying to track down a female, housetrained, non-puppy, blue roan cocker spaniel for sale.

Eventually I found one, living in Colchester, so that weekend Tom, the children, my mother, my niece and I all crammed into the Volvo and headed through the Blackwall Tunnel. Many, many hours later, we rolled up to a nondescript house, went around the back and met the most wonderful dog in the world.

Gaby was not quite two years old and had already had two litters of puppies. She had just finished nursing the last batch and the woman had decided to keep one of the puppies and let Gaby go. It was hard to understand why, because Gaby was beautiful. She had warm brown eyes with ridiculously long lashes, dangly ears that framed her face, a shiny, just-washed coat and a very gentle air. She also, looking back on it, seemed a bit vulnerable in a way that made you want to protect her. It was love at first sight.

The woman put up a very good show of being sorry that Gaby was going but it turned out that, far from being the family pet, when Gaby was not producing dogs for sale she was kept in a cage in the garden. I can still remember the children throwing a ball for her and Gaby just standing there not knowing what to do. The lady said she wasn't chasing it because it was too hot. That was odd.

We should have also found it strange when the woman said that she would post Gaby's pedigree papers to us but never asked for our address, or that she was moving house the following day but didn't know the new address. To be honest, by that time Kimberly, Christopher and my niece Mary Kate were all taking turns throwing and retrieving the ball to show Gaby how it was done, and Tom and I knew it was a done deal, despite the oddities.

We spent the entire journey home with the children in the back arguing over who got to pet Gaby's front end and who had to pet the back, while my mother was telling me that she had known all along that I would never be able to hold out. Tom, meanwhile, was driving and reminiscing about his boyhood adventures with his dog Ginger and, coincidentally, proving that men really can't do two things at once. It was a scary trip back, especially when he got to the part where Ginger swam the entire length of the Chesapeake Bay, or saved a town from flooding, or rescued a group of orphans from a burning barn. To tell you the truth, my attention was more focused on the enormous lorry that was bearing down on us as it swerved back into its own lane, with inches to spare. I was also wondering about what I had just done. Did I really need a dog?

Apparently I did, because Gaby quickly became my dog and, despite what the others may say, from the very first she loved me the most.

Loyal, sweet-natured and no trouble at all. That describes Gaby perfectly. As soon as we got her home, it became obvious that we had found ourselves a little gem. She was affectionate and appreciated everything that anyone did for her. She still, however, couldn't quite figure out how to chase balls. What she did do was wander around the house collecting the children's small stuffed animals, which she would then bring back to her basket to take care of. It was sad in a way because she was obviously missing her lost puppies, but it was also very endearing. Kimberly and Christopher were more than happy to share their toys with Gaby, but it started looking like we were going to need a bigger basket, a much bigger basket, if we didn't do something. So, after making sure that there were no new toys she could add to her collection, we started very gradually removing them until, after several months, she was left with her favourite, a little cloth doll that had come from the Winter Olympics in Lillehammer, Norway. Random, I know, but Gaby loved Dolly and that was that.

Gaby was instantly an indispensable member of the family and everyone loved her, although you won't be surprised to hear that Christopher quickly forgot that he was the one who was supposed to be doing everything for her. Within weeks, the pattern developed that Tom walked her, the children played with her and I – well, I did absolutely everything else.

As a result, Gaby and I spent a lot of time together. In fact, we went to work together every day. At that time I was the editor of the news service company Tom and I had founded and Gaby was the News Hound. Not being an overly active dog, she would spend pretty much the entire day sleeping beneath my desk, with her head on my foot. Until lunchtime, that is. Then she went off in search of her friend and our colleague Andrew, who, despite having two cats, is a true dog lover. He made sure that Gaby's water bowl was topped up, and that she always had a good supply of treats. In fact, whenever she started running out he would make a note of it and the next day a new box would arrive, strapped to the back of his bicycle.

They had their little daily routine. Gaby would wander out around 1pm and sit by Andrew's desk, staring at him. If he was in the middle of something and didn't get up quickly enough, she would then move to the doorway of the kitchen, turn around, sit down and continue to stare at him. He would eventually give in, join her in the kitchen and make their lunch. Without fail, this consisted of three sandwiches (ham and some vile-looking paste, neither one of them was particularly fussy), a few misshapen carrots (they liked organic veg), a yoghurt, an apple and a bag of crisps. They then went back to Andrew's desk and ate it in exactly the same order, every day. First came the sandwiches, which Gaby shared. Then came the yoghurt, which she didn't like so she would wander over to the other side of the room, sit down and wait. She would come back for the carrots and for three crisps, no more, no less. She would then go for a little drink while Andrew ate the apple and would swing back by his desk for the core before returning to my desk for a little post-lunch nap. The only thing that varied was the flavour of the crisps. Visitors would watch this routine and laugh; the rest of us just left them to it.

Gaby also spent a lot of time with Rory, the vet. Almost as soon as we got her home, it became apparent why her former owner (who I started to compare to the Wicked Witch of the West in *The Wizard of Oz*) was in such a hurry to get rid of her. First she developed a problem with her ears, and I found myself spending hours of my time each week cleaning them out with cotton balls and putting in some rather nasty-smelling medicine. Or perhaps it was the ears that were nasty smelling. I don't know which, but something certainly was. Even Andrew at work was beginning to notice. Apparently it was getting harder and harder for him to tell if his jar of fish paste was going off.

Rory said that Gaby wasn't the first cocker spaniel to have this problem and wouldn't be the last. It's what happens to dogs who were not designed by nature. Her big and dangly ears were perfect incubators for any germ that was hanging around on the Common. Gaby turned out to be a natural at incubation. Then it was her eyes. Her tear glands were defective and she developed dry eye, a condition which would eventually lead to blindness but could be controlled for a quite a long time by the use of some incredibly expensive eye drops that had been developed by NASA for use on the moon, or something like that. They cost £35 a tube, lasted a week and had to be picked up from the vet's every Friday. At least they worked.

Rory always said that Gaby was the world's best patient. She would let him do whatever needed doing and would lick his hand at the end. Unless what needed doing involved a needle. Then she would look at him in utter amazement that he could do such a thing to her. She never held a grudge, though.

Between her ears and her eyes, we were at the vet's fairly frequently. We had a regular standing appointment on a Friday morning when we would go in, pick up her medicine and Rory would have a quick look at her. He never charged for those check-ups. In fact, he said that they weren't really necessary once he had sorted out her ears and her eye problems were under control, but he just liked seeing her.

One of these regular Friday appointments proved memorable. I was running late and on auto-pilot, and I walked into the reception room, telling Gaby that here we were and hadn't we just had a nice walk across the Common and to say hello to everyone, when Rory came out of his office and asked me where the dog was. I suddenly realised that she wasn't there. I had left her at home. Well, that explains it. I had thought that she hadn't really been holding up her end of the conversation on the way over. Apparently they are still talking about this up at the vet's.

I have to guiltily admit that wasn't the only time I forgot Gaby. One morning on the way to work, we stopped by the bakery to pick up some bread and I tied her up outside while I popped in. Coming out of the shop, I noticed that they were filming something at the restaurant next door. It's one of those trendy places, with big picture windows, that used to be a really convenient neighbourhood bank. Now it was yet another place to get pasta. So Gaby and I spent the rest of the walk wondering about what they were filming there and bemoaning the fact that it had made a better bank than it ever did a restaurant. The day passed in the usual way, until that evening after dinner. I asked Christopher to feed the dog, while I went upstairs to get changed so I could go to the gym. I came downstairs to find Christopher standing there, holding Gaby's bowl and asking where she was. We looked all around the house. We looked in the garden. I suddenly realised that I couldn't actually remember bringing Gaby home from the office, so we went there. No Gaby. It dawned on me that I had absolutely no idea when I last saw her. I called Andrew to ask if she had had lunch with him. No, she hadn't. He hadn't said anything because I had been in a meeting all afternoon so he figured I had left her at home. I hadn't, but I started to have a sinking feeling that I knew exactly where she was.

We went back to the bakery. Of course she wasn't there. No one had seen her. We called the police and they suggested trying Battersea Dogs Home. We tried there. No answer. Everyone was crying and I was trying very hard not to feel like the worst person on the planet. I didn't succeed.

The next morning I tried calling Battersea again and they said that they had had several dogs come in the day before, so I went down and filled in the lost dog form. When it came to the section on how you had lost your dog, I felt that I had to come clean and so I wrote, 'Left outside a shop.' The incredibly sympathetic woman who works there took the form, looked at this and said, 'You have to be so careful with pedigree dogs, don't you? You just leave them outside a shop for a second and someone tries to take them.' Well, I suppose.

I joined the other people who were looking for their dogs, trying not to think about just how many seconds it was that I had left her outside the shop. We started at the top floor and worked down, going up one row of cages and down the next. They were filled with all sorts of dogs. The sound and the smell were incredible. It was like Colditz but with dogs, and kinder guards and no escape tunnels. People were gradually being reunited with their pets, until it was just me and the sympathetic lady. I was beginning to lose hope until we turned around a final corner and there she was, sitting all alone and looking totally miserable.

When she saw me, she broke into a frenzy of joy, jumping up against the bars, barking wildly, licking my hand and wagging her tail. I was so happy to see her that I would have wagged my tail myself, if I had had one. Instead I just kept petting her and telling her how sorry I was. Through the happiness and relief, I felt terrible. I had done this awful thing to her and yet she had totally and instantly forgiven me. How was I ever going to forgive myself? It hasn't been easy, especially since every few months the Dogs Home now sends me their magazine, *PAWS*. I am definitely going to have to get myself off that mailing list.

Total trust, undying devotion and utter loyalty – that awful experience showed how full to the brim Gaby was with those typical canine traits. But while she may have been your average dog in many ways, in others she was definitely unique. To say, for example, that Gaby doesn't like walking is like saying that Andy Murray doesn't like losing. Perhaps it's got something to do with being kept in a cage during your formative years (Gaby, that is, not Andy), but whatever the reason, she must be the only dog in the history of human–dog relations who would go running in the opposite direction at the sight of a lead being taken off the hook. Every walk was a battle between the forces of movement and the forces of inertia. I (or let's be honest here, Tom) would always have to pull Gaby up the road and to the Common. She would go grudgingly, every step an effort that she just didn't want to make. She would sit down every few feet and try to dig her paws in. Tom would cajole and tug. Gaby would move a little and then sit down again. Passers-by would always laugh and comment. It was pretty funny, since Tom never looked like he wanted to go for a walk much either.

This would keep up for exactly half the outing, because the second they turned around and started for home, Gaby's attitude transformed completely. She got a spring in her step, she strained at the lead, she was in a hurry to get where she was going. And where she was going was home. Gaby was too big to be a lap dog, so she settled for being a home dog. She loved her garden and her basket and her dolly and us, and just never understood the attractions of chasing squirrels, swimming in ponds or sniffing other dogs. I have to say, I'm with her on that last one.

She also didn't understand grass. For a country girl, Gaby was surprisingly urban. If she had had a motto, it would have been that there was nothing wrong with the country that concrete couldn't cure. On the Common, she stuck to the paths. On picnics, she would wait to be carried to the blanket. Luckily for her we had two patios in our garden, connected by a little stone path so she could happily wander around out there from one patio to the other, back and forth, without ever having to touch anything green.

Gaby's aversion to nature has made her famous in Cornwall. We were down visiting friends who live there one weekend and decided to walk to the pub for lunch. The humans all thought that was a great idea, as did two of the three dogs. Gaby didn't, but she was outnumbered and outvoted and was coming. The pub was, alarmingly, on the edge of a cliff and to get to it you had to walk along a path from which you were treated to a spectacular, panoramic view of sea, sky, cliffs and fields. The sun was shining, the sky was a deep blue, filled with wisps of cloud and birds, and the sea was just rough enough to be exciting. For some reason I can't quite remember, my friend had Gaby's lead. When we left the cliffs behind us and started heading across the fields, her husband let their two off and so she unclipped Gaby. Tom and I were walking up ahead. He was waxing lyrical about the beauties of nature. I was wondering how much further it was to the pub. The dogs were playing, the birds were calling, we were all laughing. Everyone was having a great time until I suddenly looked around and asked, 'Where's Gaby?' She was nowhere to be seen.

We shouted, we whistled, we worried that she had turned back and got lost, we tried not to let our thoughts linger on the cliffs, and then suddenly we heard our friend laughing, loudly. Gaby was sitting on the path, at the exact point we had left it to cross the fields, waiting patiently. She could not be moved. She had absolutely no intention of leaving the path, no matter how many bones we promised to give her when we reached the pub. There was nothing for it, we took turns carrying her. Well, Tom and John took turns, but Kate and I helped a lot by holding the lead. Everyone at the pub thought the story was hilarious. Tom and I had our picture taken, holding the dog, and there was lots of mostly good-natured banter about Londoners. I didn't mention Gaby's rural background. Why spoil a good story?

There were many other eventful walks, though there was one in particular that led to tears in our household. We were visiting friends at the time, taking Gaby with us, and Tom had taken her out for a walk. When he returned, he thought there was something wrong with her – she seemed to be even more reluctant to be out walking, and had trouble going up and down the kerb. We called a local vet who said he would be happy to have a look at her. Tom took her over and an hour later they returned. Gaby looked about the same, but it was obvious that Tom was trying very hard not to show how upset he was. The vet had said that Gaby had slipped a disc in her back and that it would be a painful, chronic condition and that the kind thing would be to put her down immediately. Tom had said that he couldn't do that, that he had to talk about it with the rest of the family and at least give us all the chance to say goodbye. The vet said that in that case, he would give her a shot of some anti-inflammatory medication which would see her through the night but, as we were due to go home that day, we should take her to our regular vet in the morning.

It was shocking; one moment the dog had a bit of a limp, the next it had become a death sentence. We really didn't know what to do – she didn't seem to be in that much pain but it was hard to tell with Gaby, she was always a very stoical sort.

We made a sad journey home and, once there, spent our time petting her, making all her favourite meals and discussing the awful decision that had to be made. Finally we decided that we couldn't be selfish, we had to do what was best for her. And so the next morning, after much crying and hugging, we said goodbye to our beloved pet and watched while Tom took her to Rory for the last time. About twenty minutes later they were back. Apparently, the shot had really helped and the disc was in place and probably hadn't been dislocated at all, or something along those lines, and we should just give her these pills every day and bring her back in a few days' time for a check-up. We did. Rory examined her from snout to tail and declared her as fit as she ever had been, while we made a mental note to never stray from our regular vet again.

We celebrated Gaby's reprieve by taking a short trip to Scotland. We had always wanted to go there and hadn't got around to it yet. But Gaby's dice with death was one of those reminders that you shouldn't always put things off, because you just never know when you are going to run into the wrong emergency vet. So we packed our bags and our bowls and headed north. We stayed in a little place outside St Andrew's. Tom looked a bit wistfully at the golf course for a minute or two, or more, but decided to join the rest of us on the beach.

The water was indescribably cold. Well, I could describe it but not without using the words 'arctic', 'numbing' and 'insanely freezing'. We built sand cities – castles with outlying buildings, we were there all afternoon – and collected stones and ran along the beach while Vangelis filled the air. Or perhaps that was just me humming. (Admit it, you're doing it now …) And all the while Gaby was with us, running in and out of the surf, digging in the sand, knocking over the castles, having a brilliant time.

That day, in particular, was a gift, an experience that we so nearly didn't get to spend together. It's just one of the many examples of how special Gaby was to our family. She was sweet-natured and affectionate and would sit for hours while you brushed her coat and chatted about your day. She appreciated everything you did for her and she never complained, not even when getting out of her bed was an effort that she really could have done without. She was always glad to see you, no matter what sort of mood you were in. Of course, she was also smelly and, more times than not, didn't quite make it out into the garden in time, but somehow that never really mattered.

In spite of her long list of ailments, she had a great life and when she wasn't at work, she was either lying in her basket with Dolly or plodding around the Common with Tom in tow. It was amazing how much they grew to look alike, each slow and steady and probably thinking about food. Or else she was sneaking out to visit the neighbours. She loved the Caseys, especially Gill. I tried not to take it personally, not even the time she jumped out of the front window, went across the road and sat down on their doorstep waiting to be let in. I told myself that it was because they had an old dog that Gaby liked playing with, but if I'm honest I think it's because she just liked hanging out there every now and then.

Despite the mortgage-trebling eye drops, Gaby's vision did deteriorate towards the end of her life, although I don't think she ever went entirely blind. She could certainly always find her bowl, her basket and her favourite toy. She could also find her way to my mother, Mema, who was going blind as well. I can still picture them sitting together on the sofa, I imagine having a great time talking about depth-perception.

Gaby started spending more and more time in her basket and only left the house for a short stroll in the garden every now and then. Rory said that she was old and creaky but as long as she was still interested in her food we should just let her enjoy herself. And she certainly was interested in food. I started making her things I thought she would like, such as steak and lamb chops and roasted chicken. Tom and Christopher wanted to know if I would feed them like that if they didn't get out of bed. No, I wouldn't. Then, just as suddenly as she took to her basket, she decided to leave it and rejoin the family. She became very affectionate and would stay by my side all the time, just waiting to be petted and fussed over. I thought it was a good sign, but Tom said that she sensed that the end was near. Sadly, it was one of those rare occasions when he was right.

A few weeks later, on a horribly rainy February day, the time I had been dreading finally arrived. My neighbour Gill came round to pick a package up that had been delivered while she was away and said she thought that there had been a dramatic decline in Gaby's health in just the few days that she had been gone. In my heart I knew she was right, although I didn't want to believe it. She stayed with me while I phoned Tom. He came right home; we wrapped Gaby up in her tartan blanket, tucked her little dolly in with her and went to see Rory. It wasn't a happy journey. When we got there Rory said that Gaby was tired and needed our help to leave. While he got ready the last needle he was ever going to give her, I stroked her head and told her to go find Mema. It was over in seconds. I imagine them together, both younger and stronger and with perfect sight. Who knows, perhaps Mom has even taught Gaby how to chase that ball.

Since then, over the course of my Pet Nanny years, there have been a few other old dogs who are no longer with us: Charlie the hound of uncertain origin who let out strange howls every now and again just to remind you that he was there; Tessie the Jack Russell terrier who spent her days in search of patches of sunlight that she could stretch out in; and Poppy the sort-of Labrador who arrived, spread out on the sofa and wouldn't move an inch for anyone. They were all great dogs.

But Gaby was special. She was my dog.

The End and the Beginning

I believe that Gaby knew how much we loved her. I certainly knew that she loved us. I just had to get through the crying and sadness and wait for the happy memories to come flooding in. I knew they would. There were so many, how could they not?

Grief is exhausting, and trying to pretend that you are not grieving is also exhausting. The world divided into 'us' and 'them'. 'Them' are kind and mean well. They say things like, 'Oh, I was sorry to hear about your dog. Are you going to be getting another one?' 'Us' say, 'I'm so sorry. It hurts so much to lose a member of the family. I know how you feel.' And they do.

I knew that Gaby was just a dog, and an old, smelly dog at that. But she was my old, smelly dog. She came into my life when my mother was alive and the children were small, and she left us when it had become mostly just me and Tom. I mourned the loss of all those years of signing paw prints on birthday cards and buying the extra little presents that came from her. I missed talking to her, and listening to the radio with her and coming down in the morning to find her waiting to start the day with me. I missed having her bowls on the floor, the ones that the children had decorated with poster paints the day we first got her, with Gaby spelled differently on each – and both differently from the spelling we eventually decided on. I even missed Dolly, probably the world's last remaining souvenir from the Lillehammer Olympics.

When Tom suggested my new Pet Nanny career, I wasn't sure. I knew that I wasn't ready for another dog of our own. I don't think he was either. But we both realised that we missed having a dog and that the house was lacking some vital component that only a dog could bring. It's more than love or happiness. It's a wholehearted joy in just being alive that is rare in people, but standard issue in dogs.

Because of Gaby and in recognition of how much she added to our lives, we decided to say yes – to a new life of dogs and their owners, of wagging tails and tall tales, of merriment and mirth and mud. That was her legacy to us.

And so Serena entered our lives. They say one person can change your life and she was definitely in that category.

As the head of a Pet Nanny service, it is Serena's job to deal with owners tortured by guilt because they are abandoning a treasured family member as they depart on an exotic holiday. She finds the nannies who will look after, care for and love their charges, but never enough to make these dogs dig in their paws and refuse to return home. She frequently has to deal with people who have lost touch with the fact that their dog is actually a dog. Serena also has to convince the nannies that a six-month-old puppy who is not quite housetrained and chews constantly is the perfect companion for an elderly dog who needs help standing up on wooden floors.

Like much senior management, Serena doesn't actually work at the coal face. She rules from a distance and only intervenes if two dogs don't get along, or if a nanny falls ill – or is suddenly invited to Hawaii. She normally doesn't meet the owners, or the pets, and does her liaising, co-ordinating and persuading via email or over the phone. Her online form covers everything from the dog's breed, date of birth and vet details to its current vaccination status and situation vis-à-vis fleas and worms.

The final section asks the owner to explain anything else we should know about their dog. In every owner's mind their dog is always lovely, well-behaved, friendly and obedient. One or two will chew but only if left alone in a dark, soundproof room for weeks, without a chew toy. None will wrench your shoulder out of its socket when attempting to mug a squirrel, skirt around a sea of toys to gnaw on the antique silk rug that your ancestor brought back from China, or howl at the moon. None are allowed on the furniture or up the stairs, where they might be tempted to crawl into your bed. These euphemistic assessments often fall apart when I begin asking questions at my initial meet-up with potential clients.

Serena knows that Pet Nannies are born, not made. Applications are not accepted. You have to be asked to join her ranks. At our first meeting, she suggested that assuming this position would give me a chance to enjoy caring for wonderful dogs without all the obligations of ownership. At the end of it, she made it clear that she felt I was the perfect hire. After all, if I could handle difficult people in countries saddled with 850 languages, it would be easy to communicate with the dogs of others, and their occasionally eccentric owners. Who was I to question her infinite wisdom?

And so through Serena I found my new career, the thing I was born to do. From the moment she first asked me if I would like to watch someone's dog over a weekend, I started enjoying that part of life more and more. Not only that, but I was good at it. I understood the dogs and I understood the owners. Lateral thinking, negotiating skills, flexibility, knowing what to say and what not to say, juggling conflicting interests, being able to see things from another angle – all skills that are important in a diplomat, essential in a Pet Nanny. I realised that all those years of diplomacy were going to come in handy. All those years of having, and loving, dogs could be put to good use. The fact that I could live with chaos and disorder and noise wasn't going to hurt either.

As I began my career, Serena taught me that one of the pleasures of being a Pet Nanny is working with the owners.

Some owners believe a dog is a nice addition to life. Others think a dog is an essential part of the family. Finally, there are those who are convinced that dogs are human beings.

As you may have guessed, Pet Nannies specialise in the latter.

Of course, those who believe a dog is a dog would check him into a kennel before going on holiday. But if you consider Lassie one of the children, there is no way you can go off on holiday unless you are sure that she is safely with the grandparents or a qualified Pet Nanny, chewing quality bones and catching balls on a dead run.

Our clientele love their dogs. Many have already raised their families and brought dogs into their homes after their children have moved away. No empty nests for these families.

They worry about their dogs, have them properly vaccinated, make sure they take their vitamins, and include their names on all holiday cards. That's why they arrive at the Pet Nanny's door with beds and balls and treats and toys and the many other things they think their boy or girl will be missing from home. They also leave a long list of contact numbers, instructions, suggestions and, without fail, little goodies to be handed out in case their pet starts fretting.

Sometimes they are young couples trying to learn what it's like caring for a child. Of course, they acknowledge that dogs are not the same as children but frequently they surround their pets with many of the accoutrements of toddlers. While this may sound silly, the fact is that dogs give them the feeling of parenthood without worrying about the cost of university fees. In addition to couples who have decided not to have children, there are dog-crazy gay partners, widows and widowers looking for a sound reason to get out of the house, and parents who want to teach their children responsibility. All have love to spare.

Despite their many differences in age, dietary habits, religion or lack thereof, they are world-class worriers. They worry about Roux's tummy while watching the sun set at the Taj Mahal, or Ella's diet while hiking in the Alps, or Alfie's ears while swimming in the Red Sea. They worry that Charlie is so badly behaved that he won't be allowed to return, or that he will love the Pet Nanny's house so much he won't want to leave.

They phone, they email, they text, they Facebook, they tweet, they even mail postcards from all over the world. They call to tell Frankie that they found him a wonderful present in Berlin. They email Barney to reassure him that he would have found Tunisia unbearably hot. They contact Lily to update her on the progress of renovations at the Menorca house and reassure her that she will love the view from the balcony.

They also send photos. Daily. From holiday dinner tables, poolside lounge chairs and seaside sand castles. And they love receiving pictures of their dog wearing a Christmas hat while sitting beneath the tree, or fast asleep on a lap, or sprinting through a field.

As the sort of owner who always worried about my own dog when we had to leave her behind, I understand. Was she being good? Were the people looking after her remembering her ear drops? Did they understand that she couldn't sleep without her little stuffed toy? Did she miss me? It's not easy being a dog owner, especially when you must trust your animal to someone you barely know.

Which brings me to the dogs …

Hector

Eileen,

I have an eleven-month-old silver grey, short-haired
Weimaraner named Hector. Elisabeth and Max have just
moved here from Paris and need someone to look after him
for a few days. He enjoys walking and playing with sticks,
can be somewhat greedy and has no road sense. Elisabeth
will call to arrange a meeting.

Regards,

Serena

And so it began, with Hector the Weimaraner.

I know, I had no idea what a Weimaraner was either, but
it turns out that they are those large, grey dogs with amber-
coloured eyes, most often seen wearing hats and playing poker
in posters. They were originally used by royalty to hunt game
such as boar, bear and deer, which explains why Hector was
living in a south London flat.

He and his friends, Elisabeth and Max, came around one
afternoon for a cup of tea and a play in the garden. Well, everyone did at least one of those things. I have to say that they were
a very nice trio. Elisabeth would say things like, '*Ça suffit 'Ector*',
while Max told him to drop the stick. I quickly realised that the
dog was bilingual when he ignored them both and continued
to chew his way through my entire wood pile. Being new to
this, I wasn't really sure what they were looking for in a nanny
for their pet. I must have passed the test, though, because it
was eventually decided that Hector would be happy to be a

temporary member of the family and that he would soon be returning for a brief stay.

A few days later Hector duly arrived, along with his bed, crate, food, toys, treats, towels, shampoo and the million other things necessary for a dog to spend a couple of days away from home. After a rather long period of time, during which Elisabeth and Max beat themselves up about the fact that they were leaving the dog behind, the two of them finally left. I was alone with my first charge.

I so wish I could say that everything went well.

It certainly started off well. Hector and I went for a nice walk on the Common, where he made friends with the local dogs while I chatted to their owners and tried my best to be a credit to the Pet Nanny service. It was one of those amazingly sunny days and I rather thought that I was pulling it off. Hector was beautiful, sleek, stylish and athletic, although while watching him run, I realised that I would need a whole new wardrobe if I were to have any hope of being mistaken for the owner of a Weimaraner.

Things started to go downhill on the way home. Hector was becoming a bit too interested in a pile of something unidentifiable and, remembering his billing as being somewhat greedy, I quickly put him on his lead and pulled him away. At that exact moment he spied a squirrel, realised that his chances of encountering boar, bear or deer were somewhat slim, and took off after it in a way that would have made those royal huntsmen proud. Unfortunately, as Hector had also been advertised as having absolutely no road sense, I reluctantly decided that I couldn't let go of the lead. Instead I grimly held on and shouted 'Ça suffit 'Ector', or words to that effect. They had no effect. Luckily the squirrel eventually went up a tree and while Hector ran around it barking like a mad thing, I tried to put my arm back in its socket.

By the time we got home my shoulder felt better but my back had completely given up the unequal struggle of dealing with a large, grey, royal hunting dog and so, after a brief stop for some aspirin for me and some water for him, I took my heating pad and went to bed.

Not very many minutes later the hunting dog arrived looking, it must be said, very sorry for himself and proceeded to put his nose on the bed. I didn't say anything, which he took as a good sign and before long he started to inch forward until his whole head was on the bed. I ignored him and soon his neck and shoulders joined us, and then the tip of one paw. He was watching me the whole time, with a suitably pathetic expression on his face and hope in his heart. The other paw arrived. He continued looking at me and inching forward. The whole thing had taken well over half an hour by this point and we still had most of the back half to go. One back paw popped on, and soon afterwards the other. The tail brought up the rear. Then the assault on the middle of the bed began. By the time he was finished, Hector was completely stretched out in the absolute centre of the bed while my heating pad and I were hanging on to the edge and I was trying desperately hard not to laugh. It hurt too much.

We spent the rest of the day lying down and telling each other how awful we felt, which made for a very bonding experience. Well, I told Hector and he didn't disagree so I assumed that he felt the same way. It was so comforting to have company. I tried very hard not to dwell on the fact that he was the reason I had taken to my bed, and instead thought about what might be the matter with him. I didn't have long to wait before I found out.

The next morning I woke up, went downstairs and discovered fifteen separate 'incidents'. Hector had thrown up on every single cushion of both sofas, two throw pillows and the rug in three places. Not to mention the three separate spots in his basket. Or the other rug. An hour later the house was somewhat clean, although I still smelled of dog vomit, despite having scrubbed off most of my skin.

Elisabeth and Max arrived to find Hector sitting in the midst of all the chaos looking as if he had just arrived and had absolutely no idea what was going on. They quickly assured me that Hector had only been sick twice in his entire life, despite the fact that he had swallowed some of the amniotic fluid when he was born and, according to the specialist vet he goes to in Essex, was thought to have an auto-immune problem. What?! I suppose that explained the rash that was slowly developing on his tummy. At least it probably meant that he wasn't allergic to me. That's something, I suppose.

And so we all spent a half hour or so looking at the rash and trying to ignore everything else in the room before the three of them eventually headed home to Clapham, leaving me to deal with the cushions and to reflect on the joys of being a Pet Nanny. As I steered around the damp patches in search of more aspirin, I wondered if I was cut out for this life. The last time I had injured my back in the line of duty was while fleeing from mutineering fishermen on an American tuna boat, somewhere in the South China Sea, in the middle of the night. And back then all I had to do was run – cleaning up was definitely not required. So after my first canine guest had departed, I had to ask myself some important questions. Was I adventurous enough to face the unknown and handle whatever the job threw at me? Was I willing to sacrifice the wellbeing of my body and my household furnishings? Could I still run if required? And would I ever agree to have Hector back to stay? I really only knew the answer to the last question – absolutely. A doleful expression and a waggly tail will get you a long way in life (although next time his owners are paying for a carpet cleaner – I may be soft, but I am not an idiot).

So when the next email arrived, I was willing to try another …

Vita

Hector was a beautiful looking dog, if you overlooked the rash of course, but he couldn't hold a candle to Vita. Not even if he had thumbs.

Hi Eileen,

I have a six-month-old Pomeranian named Vita. She's a rather posh pup, her mother (or maybe it was her father) was a Crufts champion! She is housetrained, loves company, going for walks and playing with other dogs. Chews a bit. Are you up for it?

Love,

Serena

'Vita,' I was informed by her owner Michael when they came over to meet me (and, as it turned out, to inspect my house) 'is Latin for "life" and we named her that because she is very lively.' 'That's a lovely name,' I said, and happily managed not to not add, 'but in that case why didn't you name her "Vivax", since it's Latin for lively?' Somehow I just knew that Michael was not the kind of person who would find Latin one-upmanship amusing.

What Michael was, was a man totally besotted by his dog. And who could blame him? Vita was absolutely beautiful and it wasn't at all hard to believe the Crufts connection (it was her grandfather, by the way). She was also somewhat quiet for such a young dog, which was a bit odd. I soon learned why.

It quickly became obvious that Michael was serious about training – very serious. Vita must always walk on the left, no more than half a step ahead of or behind the walker. She must sit at every corner and wait to be told 'come'. She must not run after other dogs but must wait to be told 'play'. I'm not entirely sure what was supposed to happen when she encountered squirrels; perhaps sit and wait to be told 'chase' or 'ignore' or 'eat'? Among many other things, she could also not jump up on people, sit down on furniture or behave in a 'beastly' way. You get the general idea.

After a quick cup of tea, Michael wanted to look around the house to make sure that it was nice enough for the granddaughter of a Crufts champion to stay in. Well, that's the impression I got, although he said that it was to make sure there was nothing dangerous that could hurt Vita. After assuring himself that there was no bleach waiting to be drunk, knives waiting to be licked or lead paint waiting to be chewed, Michael wanted to see the garden.

Usually when people see our garden for the first time, they are amazed at how big it is for London, surprised by what a keen gardener Tom is, pleased by how pretty it looks. Not Michael. He was looking for danger. After some intensive searching, he concluded that we had no pond that Vita could drown in, no pit that she could fall into, no diseased tree limbs that were waiting to crush her and no crazed hedgehogs waiting to attack. We did, however, have rose bushes. These, he informed me, have thorns. Those thorns, apparently, could damage Vita in some truly horrific but unspecified way. Would I consider chopping them down? Ummmm … no, I wouldn't. After a somewhat awkward silence, I did say that I would get Tom to tie them up, back, away. Michael settled for that, not entirely happily.

After such a bizarre first meeting, you may wonder why I let Vita come. The fact that she was just so lovely to look at must have had something to do with it, as did the fact that she was so amazingly well-behaved. How much trouble could she be?

The answer was – quite a lot.

Vita may have had Michael fooled, but she really was a puppy after all. She was affectionate, energetic and full of life. She was also full of sharp teeth and mischief. Once Michael was safely off the property, Vita let rip. I soon gave up trying to make her walk on the left, sit at corners, stay off furniture and pretty much everything else. I was too busy cleaning up after her, rescuing things from her jaws, throwing away the things that I didn't rescue in time, hoovering and trying to get her to stop biting my ankles.

In one memorable ten-minute period, while I was concentrating on writing an email and not paying her enough attention, she ate Tom's wallet. To be precise, not the whole wallet, just large chunks of it. Luckily she missed the credit cards. She also got my favourite pen, although I was happy to note that it had fought back bravely and left ink all over her mouth and paws. Lastly she managed to chew and, since I never found them again, presumably swallow parts of the remote control. Not anything that was essential for its operation, as long as you don't mind holding it together and jiggling it every time you want to turn on the television or change a channel.

By the end of Vita's stay, I was counting down the hours until Michael's return. Between the stress of keeping the descendant of a Crufts champion safe from my house, and keeping my house safe from the descendant of a Crufts champion, I was completely exhausted. But even so, Vita, or Ryvita as we called her when Michael wasn't around, was an absolutely great dog. Her enthusiasm for life was infectious and her love of mischief was totally forgivable. She was, after all, a puppy.

As I said goodbye to Vita, I began to realise that to be a good Pet Nanny you had to honestly care about your charges, and that if you cared, you were vulnerable. You had no say about when you would see a dog you were fond of again, if ever. They came into your life, they found a comfortable place in your heart and then they were off and delighted to be going back home with their owner, which I always find hard not to take to heart. I secretly wish they'll look back at me as they go or display some reluctance to leave me.

On the other hand, I was definitely beginning to enjoy having dogs back in the house – there was no doubt that with Kimberly at university in Scotland and her brother at boarding school in Kent, the house was feeling empty. Not only were they gone, but so was all their noise, and their clutter and their enthusiasms. The house was clean – well, cleanish – and quiet, and Tom and I both hated it. But at the same time, I was nervous about getting attached to all these temporary pets, who might never return to my care. In the end it was Tom, a glass-half-full kind of person even when there is no glass, who convinced me to concentrate on all the new dogs who would enter our lives, and so my Pet Nanny career began to flourish.

Vita was one who came back often after her first visit and was always welcome, but the last time I saw her, she was walking on Michael's left and, for once, did actually look sadly back over her shoulder at me. I was sad too. They were moving to the country the following week, so that was to be her last stay with us. But there were plenty of new dogs waiting to take her place.

Rafa

Rafa was Roxana's first pet. She obviously wanted a pony as a child.

Hi Eileen,

Me again. Just wondering if you'd be interested in a lovely, seven-month-old, medium-sized chocolate labradoodle called Rafa. He is very well trained, doesn't pull (not allowed to!), doesn't fight, comes to his name and whistle, good on commands, loves ragging with other dogs, likes affection but isn't demanding. Not keen on getting into a car, but fine once he's in! Any chance you'd like to meet? Let me know when you can.

Love

S x

Labradoodles are very popular in this neighbourhood. You used to see one or two every now and again but suddenly they seem to be every third dog up on the Common. As far as I could tell before looking after one, they are small and friendly, have beautiful cream-coloured wavy coats, and a Labrador's love of life tempered by a poodle's sense of their own self-importance. Or at least I thought that until I met Rafa.

Obviously the result of two genetically engineered dogs having met one dark evening, Rafa is, quite simply, the biggest, brownest dog in the world. If Central Casting put out a call for a shaggy dog to play the best friend of some lovable street urchin, Rafa would, without a shadow of a doubt, get the part.

He has a rough coat that you could use to wipe up industrial spills, a tail that could knock over a medium-sized van and a personality that could light up the universe. He was consistently voted 'Dog of the Month' up at the office and, believe me, they had quite a few dogs to choose from. Rafa is named after the tennis player, and he and Nadal do seem to share many qualities. They are both scarily strong, slightly odd-looking, firm favourites with the crowd, like chasing balls, enjoy being on grass and don't listen to whistles.

One day Rafa and his owner, a very small and slim woman, came over for a get-to-know-you cup of tea, accompanied by a large bag filled with an assortment of dog products. Roxana is by nature a very athletic person but, due to a back injury, has been forced to give up competitive sports. In order to stay active and keep her back in order, she has taken to walking. Naturally enough, she wanted a companion to do it with and, after a bit of research up on the Common, made the same assumption about labradoodles as I did. That may have been a mistake for a person with a bad back.

It soon became apparent that Roxana had never owned a dog before in her life and had leapt in at the deep end. She proceeded to tell me how well trained Rafa was and showed me the whistle he came to and the spray collar he had, but no longer needed, to prevent him from jumping up on people. She told me how at mealtimes he sat while his bowl was put down and waited for the command 'take it' before eating, how he walked to heel and how he could be stopped from barking by seeing you raise one finger to your lips. This was all incredibly impressive. Of course, it would have been even more impressive if Rafa had not been lying at her feet while she was telling me this, trying to gnaw the leg off my coffee table.

Roxana should have told me a few more things, such as that: he doesn't eat the chicken you have left defrosting on the draining board in the kitchen; he won't wrench your arm out of its socket if he happens to be on the lead when he sees a squirrel; he will go up stairs without having one person pull him from the front while another pushes him from behind; and his enthusiasm levels cannot be measured on the Richter scale, because none of those things were true either.

It was, however, true that Rafa did not like getting into cars. One particularly sunny day, we decided to take him to Wimbledon Common as a little treat and so got out the instructions on 'How to get Rafa into a car'. We read them through. First you have to unwrap the pepperoni stick (which comes supplied with the dog), then open the back door of the car on the driver's side. Next you get in and slide a quarter of the way across the seat. Your assistant then brings Rafa to the open door. You tear off a small piece of pepperoni and put it on the edge of the seat, nearest the door. Rafa sniffs it, takes it, eats it. You then slide a little further across the seat and put down another piece of meat. Rafa eases his head further in and takes it. You slide across further and put more pepperoni down. Rafa eases in further and eats it. This continues until you are touching the passenger-side door and most of Rafa is inside the car.

You then quickly leap out, firmly closing the door behind you, while your assistant shoves the remaining bits of Rafa into the car and slams the door shut.

Christopher, home for the weekend, and I thought that we had this down to a tee and so we began. I got in the car and unwrapped the pepperoni. I put it down. Rafa ate it. I slid over and put some more down, Rafa stood by the car door and stared at the pepperoni. Then he stared at me. Then he sat down. I got out and we tried once more. It happened again. Finally, after about ten minutes, Christopher said, 'Get out of the car and give me the pepperoni.' I did. He then bent down, picked Rafa up, put him in the back of the car, unwrapped the rest of the pepperoni and ate it himself.

Rafa was not an easy dog to walk either, not even for Tom who is tall and fairly strong. One day they came back from an early morning reconnaissance of squirrel levels, with Rafa ready to go right back out on patrol and Tom rubbing his arm. Apparently Rafa had forgotten to mention that he wanted to be instantly on the other side of the road, and caught Tom unawares. Still, no harm was done. Later, Tom went to put the rubbish out for collection. He reached down to lift the bag, clutched his chest and said, 'You better call an ambulance.' Ten minutes later the paramedics were hooking him up to monitors and he was being rushed off to hospital for further tests. I followed in the car and arrived to find him in the cardiac intensive care unit, with tubes and wires coming out of him from all over the place and machines blinking and beeping ominously. After several hours of having dye injected into his veins and cameras sent up his arteries and who knows what done with all those vials of blood they had taken, it was determined that he had not had a heart attack after all and was sent off for chest X-rays. More poking and prodding followed. Eventually, after some very scary hours and more than a few terrible cups of hospital coffee, we learned that he had cracked a rib when Rafa pulled him over. Still, at least we had an exciting day, and found out that Tom has a remarkably good heart for a man his age.

Without a doubt, if Rafa was human he would one day find himself standing in a hoodie in a dock while his mother told everyone who would listen what a wonderful boy he was. And the truth of the matter is, she would be right. He *is* a wonderful boy, just an outstandingly naughty one.

However, as we're a forgiving family when it comes to mischief-makers, Rafa became a regular guest and soon we had all fallen in love with him – even Kimberly who normally doesn't like dogs unless they're stuffed or in a bun with ketchup. There's something unbelievably comforting about him. He's the dog you want in your corner when the world is beating down on you, when the dentist wants to pull the tooth you just wanted him to look at, when the staff are being difficult and the family are absent. He's the one who made me realise how much a dog can contribute to your life, giving it a rhythm and a routine and, most importantly, making you part of your community. If you're an elderly widow, a dog gives you the opportunity to go out walking and talking to people. If you're facing retirement, you have company as you ponder the next stage of life. To people without children, a dog is someone to love. To people with children, he's someone extra to love. A dog gives young mothers the hope that someone will always listen to them and never have temper tantrums, and to children, he is the playmate who is always willing to play. For a Pet Nanny? Well, for this Pet Nanny at least, they are a way to deal with the loss of your own dog when you just aren't ready to bring a new member of the family into your home. And, this being England, they are also an excellent way to turn strangers into friends.

So for me, Rafa was the real point of no return, when I couldn't imagine going back to a dog-less existence.

Ella

Rafa may have been naughty but nice, but Ella was just plain nice.

Hi Eileen,

I have a very nice two-and-a-half-year-old black Lab who is well-mannered, housetrained, friendly, loves children, chasing sticks and going for walks. She doesn't bark, doesn't pull on the lead and is no trouble at all. I was wondering if you'd be up for a meet?!?

Love

S xx

Having so far encountered a run of mischievous dogs, however endearing they may have been, I was definitely ready for 'well-mannered'. Training in the diplomatic service only prepares you for so much. That being said, their tricks were not nearly as trying as some of the characters I used to deal with back in my public service days. Such encounters had given me a deep-felt and sincere admiration for people who are able to work with the public without causing them bodily harm. No dog has ever asked me the name of a flower they once saw in Hyde Park that was yellow. Or possibly pink. Nor has a dog ever demanded that I pay for her passport photo because the photographer made her look fat. No, in general I was much happier confronting the challenges presented by dogs but still, there are only so many lead tug-of-wars you can handle and soft furnishings you can replace before you again start to question the wisdom of your new career choice. So Ella was a very welcome change of pace for someone still finding their feet in the Pet Nanny service.

'Nice' – that's the word that describes Ella perfectly. Her best friend was Duckie, a remarkably lifelike stuffed creature who went everywhere with her. On the rare occasions that they weren't found together, the question 'Where's Duckie?' always made her look around anxiously and you could just tell that she was thinking, 'Oh no, where *is* Duckie?!' Luckily he was never missing for long, which was just as well because I would have hated it if Ella was upset. She was too nice, and much too soft.

Besides Duckie, the other big love in Ella's life was going out for walks, which was rather surprising when you considered that she was a bit on the large side. Not enormous, but what we used to call 'chunky' in my childhood days. It was probably because she didn't burn up that many calories on her outings – she was much too slow for that. With other dogs, a walk didn't actually mean a walk. It meant a mad run, an enthusiastic romp with other dogs, a frenzied chase of squirrels, a quick dip in the pond, a splash in a muddy puddle. But with Ella, a walk meant a walk, and usually a fairly sedate one at that, so perhaps she wasn't quite the most suitable dog for Tom to have taken on the day he did his sponsored walk around Richmond Park.

I dropped the two of them off early on a drizzly autumn morning. Tom was armed with his Cub Scout-issue rain poncho. Ella had just her regular coat on. Duckie took one look at the weather and decided to stay with me. They set off with a cheery wave to conquer the fifteen-mile trek around the park, carrying so much food with them that the danger of getting lost and starving to death was not going to be an issue. My last sight of them was of two slow and steady types, trudging off into the distance and not seeming to care how long it took them.

It took them a very long time. I came back hours later to meet them at the exact spot from which they had set off. It was, after all, a circular walk. After a wait so ridiculously long that I was beginning to think of sending out the park rangers, I suddenly saw two sodden creatures emerging from the mist. One of them was carrying an enormous tree trunk in their mouth.

Apparently Ella had found a massive log right near the beginning of the journey, picked it up and wouldn't let go of it, except for short snack breaks, for the entire day, which is an incredible feat when you come to think about it. I was very impressed and told her so, several times. Tom, on the other hand, was less impressed as, he explained, Ella had been holding this thing at exactly knee height, so that he had to spend the entire walk trying not to get bowled over. I'm not sure how he thinks that simply not falling down is on a par with carrying an enormous tree trunk around in your mouth, for hours. Honestly, men.

Despite her repeated attempts to take him down though, Ella and Tom really bonded that day and while he will never replace Duckie in her affections, it was obvious that she enjoyed his company as much as he did hers. They have gone on many walks together since then and although none has been as long, or as wet, or has raised as much money for charity, they have all been 'nice'. There's a lot to be said for that.

Elvis and Vegas

While Ella was willing to walk for hours in Richmond Park, it has to be said that her favourite haunt is our very own Common. She's not alone, but while there may be millions of dogs up on Wandsworth Common, I can guarantee you that only two of them are called Elvis and Vegas, and it's not just their names that are special.

Hi Eileen,

Just been speaking to a nice lady who has come down from Manchester to live with her fella in Clapham, bringing her two mini schnauzers called Elvis and Vegas!!

They are going to a trainer to stop them from pulling on the lead and barking/chewing so should be fine on all three, don't fight with other dogs, or chew (apart from Elvis and socks). They come to their names, are not greedy, don't yap, will play with other dogs, like affection and love being around people. What do you think?

Regards,

Serena

By the time Elvis and Vegas arrived in my life, I and the rest of the household were getting into the swing of this Pet Nanny thing. I did the paperwork, handled all relations with the owners and spent a great deal of time filling food and water bowls. Tom did the early morning walks and we both took them to the office during the day where they, mostly, sat quietly at our feet under the desk. In the evening, we lay on the sofa with our hands dangling over the side, scratching a piece of fur. The children came and went, much like the dogs, and we gradually settled in to our new routine, shaping our lives around our charges. And despite the new demands on my time, we carried on with our everyday lives – I even managed to get my black belt in karate.

I'm not just randomly dropping that into the conversation, although I have to admit that I really do enjoy mentioning it every now and again. No, I am telling you because the following day, I received the email about Elvis and Vegas, which came as a complete surprise. I had assumed, as the only certified martial artist on the entire Pet Nanny register, that I would be immediately overwhelmed with requests to take care of Dobermanns and pit bulls. That was in the days, of course, before I realised that there were no Dobermanns or pit bulls enrolled in the service. We deal more in Labradors and Portuguese water dogs and Tibetan terriers and, it seems, miniature schnauzers. That was also in the days before I realised that, unassuming as they may sound, having a black belt in karate comes in handy when dealing with Elvis and Vegas.

I should mention that my brother has a Maltipoo named Presley and, I'm really not kidding here, an 'Elvis Room' in his house, so I took their names right in my stride. After all, I figured that I was pretty much used to this insanity. I was wrong.

Upon their arrival with owner Jo, the first thing I noticed about the pair is that Elvis looked exactly like those Kaiser Wilhelm posters you used to see in all the old movies (or would have if Kaiser Wilhelm had been a small, grey dog), while Vegas was enormously fat. There's no other way to put it. She was totally spherical, with tiny little legs and a tummy that was in danger of scraping the floor. She looked, in fact, a lot like Elvis did in his Vegas days, which was useful in a way as it meant that I wouldn't have any trouble remembering who was who. Vegas was wearing a shiny pink collar with cut-out flowers on it that reminded me of when I was younger and heavier and my mother used to put big bows in my hair. It wasn't a good look, then or now, but Vegas didn't seem to mind. She was much too busy dashing – well not quite dashing, but going pretty quickly for someone her size – out into the garden to bark furiously at whatever it was she thought was out there. Elvis, meanwhile, lifted his leg and piddled on my sofa. I was already wondering if Jo could get a refund from the dog trainer.

Jo, by the way, soon became one of my favourite owners. Very glam in an athletic sort of way, she was a personal trainer interested in alternative things, like neural linguistic programming and visualisation and lots of other techniques that I pretended to understand but didn't. She was also enormously generous with her time and knowledge. In fact, when I was doing the London to Paris bike ride, she spent hours outside my house, defending her car from the traffic warden and giving me advice on nutrition and training. She had only recently moved to London to be with her boyfriend, Chris, a man who was willing to spend a great deal of money to make sure that other people had the dogs as often as possible. I can't quite figure out if he didn't like dogs in general or just these two in particular, whom, it turned out, he had nicknamed 'The Evil One' and 'Doughnut Belly'. Why did I not pick up on the signs?

Anyway, Jo reassured me that the beasties would be very well-behaved and headed off. Shortly after, I decided to take them up to the Common … or at least, I tried to. As soon as I got their leads out, Vegas went into a frenzy and started trying to eat Elvis's back leg. It was as if he had suddenly turned into a giant chicken kiev and somebody had just poured the garlic butter on. I was beginning to seriously worry about whether Vegas started at the back and then munched her way forward and whether there used to be another sibling, Nashville or maybe Graceland. But Elvis was looking fairly unconcerned, so I guessed that Vegas chewed a bit but didn't actually swallow.

Once she had stopped gnawing on her brother, we tried again for the Common. As soon as we got there I took off their leads, at which point Elvis immediately made a mad dash for freedom and was last seen heading across the bridge and over to the pond. I knew that one of the many things this anonymous trainer had supposedly taught them was to respond to their names, but I just couldn't bring myself to start shouting 'Elvis' across the Common, so I staggered after him, carrying his fifty-pound sister and asking everyone if they had seen a small dog who looked like Kaiser Wilhelm. As you can imagine, this approach wasn't very successful and so, with no other choice, I reluctantly started yelling, 'Elvis! Elvis, where are you?', at which point a passing jogger stopped in his tracks, slowly walked back to me, shook his head and in a sad voice said, 'He's dead.' It was going to be a long weekend.

Of course, it was a much longer weekend for Yoda, the young lurcher who also came to stay later that day. Elvis took an instant and intense dislike to him and chased him out into the garden, where Vegas was busy barking at anything that moved. Poor Yoda, who had until that point been leading a quiet life, really didn't know what to do and soon resembled a ping pong ball that was being belted back and forth. Every time he went near the door, Elvis growled. Every time he went further into the garden, Vegas barked. Finally he just decided to sit down and pretend he was somewhere else, which wasn't really a long-term solution. After a while, I simply had to admit defeat, phone Serena and ask her to look after him for the rest of the weekend. I could swear that Elvis actually smirked when he heard that.

After seeing off Yoda, the dogs had a great time. We went to watch Christopher play rugby, although I'm not sure that having his parents turn up with miniature schnauzers named Elvis and Vegas was such a good idea, particularly as both made sure everyone was aware of their presence. Vegas disgraced herself when she tried to eat the rugby ball, whereas Elvis got into the kit bag and ran across the pitch with several socks in his mouth, and several boys chasing after him trying to retrieve them. Looking back now, I suppose it was rather funny, really.

Other than that, they haven't been too bad as house guests, apart from a few memorable incidents such as the time Vegas wandered off while Tom was walking her. He ran around in ever-increasing circles, he called her, he searched the under-growth and, this being Vegas, around all the bins, but he just couldn't find her. Eventually he came home to enlist my help in the hunt. Unfortunately, when he arrived I was standing in the front doorway chatting to a man who had heard about Pet Nanny and wanted to know more about it. I was in full flow and enthusiastically telling him what a wonderful service it was, when Tom loomed up behind him and started an amazingly good impersonation of someone doing charades for the film *Missing*. When he did the big belly sign, I guessed that it had something to do with Vegas, which was kind of confusing since she was standing right behind him watching the whole performance. Tom, a man who can normally find humour in anything, was for some reason not amused.

When you name dogs Elvis and Vegas, you have to expect them to have some character and these two don't disappoint. They are incredibly naughty but they are also very lovable and great fun, and I think they are wonderful. It's a minority opinion. Looking back on the description Serena gave me of them, I must say that it wasn't really a total misrepresentation – Elvis does like chewing socks and they both love affection. Just make sure that Vegas doesn't catch you when you are lying on the sofa. It can be remarkably painful as she tries to curl up on your stomach – like having someone drop a bowling ball on you from a great height. But please don't tell Jo that. She seems to think that Vegas is losing weight. I guess that's what practising visualisation techniques can do for you.

I've come to know Elvis and Vegas very well, mainly because they are here so much. Jo does a lot of residential courses, leaving Chris and the dogs at home alone. That lasts, on average, perhaps half an hour before he gets into his car and pops them round. He says that they will be happier here, which is probably true, but doesn't explain the huge smile on his face as he drives away.

Harrison

Elvis and Vegas may have caused quite a stir up on the Common, but at least they realised that it was a Common, and that they were basically city dogs. Not Harrison.

Hi Eileen,
I have a wonderful Chesapeake Bay retriever named Harrison. He is just over a year old, with a lovely temperament. Good with children and other dogs, pulls a bit on the lead, loves chasing sticks and muddy puddles. Will you meet?
Love,
Serena

How could I not want to meet Harrison? Tom's grandfather had a farm on the Chesapeake Bay and we have all been subjected to (I mean fascinated by) his 'boyhood summers on the farm' stories for years, in glorious detail. I already knew all about the migrating geese and the correct way to carry a shotgun (broken and pointing down – you never know, you might need that information some day, although I'm fairly certain that I never will), about the dogs with mouths so soft they could carry an egg but who usually carried downed birds instead and, of course, about the joys of eating something that was just minding its own business and trying to get to Florida before you blasted it out of the sky.

So I agreed to meet Harrison and a few days later Melanie, her toddler daughter, baby son and the Hound of the

Baskervilles all appeared at my front door. Harrison was a deep chocolate brown, with broad shoulders and a rear that somehow seemed higher than his front. He easily came up to my waist, which was handy because that made it much easier to see his amazing coat – it was thick and woven and reminded me of those baskets you see on holiday that have been made out of plaited palm leaves and are remarkably watertight. He seemed like a very nice dog; in fact, they seemed like a very nice family and appeared to get on well together, despite the differences in size. Melanie was pleased to meet someone who knew so much about the Chesapeake Bay; although in retrospect she probably didn't need to see all those family photos of the farm. Anyway, we decided that Harrison would spend his time with us while they went off to Barbados. I was a tad jealous but Harrison didn't seem to mind – perhaps he knew that they don't have geese in the Caribbean anyway.

A few days later Harrison arrived, accompanied by a tall, powerfully built Scotsman who, I have to say, looked like he was far better suited to the family dog than the rest of the family. After a bit of affectionate thumping of his dog, he left, Harrison settled down and I started wondering why my sitting room suddenly looked like it belonged in a doll's house.

Harrison was obviously a smart dog because he quickly figured out where the absolute centre of the room was, laid down on it and stretched out. It made life somewhat hard since the exact centre of the room turned out to be the one spot you had to go through to get anywhere else in the house. That was something I hadn't realised before. But his overwhelming presence wasn't all bad since it meant that while he was with us I didn't have to feel guilty about not going to the gym – all that climbing over him every time I wanted to go somewhere had to be good exercise. It turned out to be much more of a workout than that machine where your legs go up and down while your arms go back and forth. Getting over Harrison without getting maimed required co-ordination, conditioning and courage. The trick was timing your climb so that you could get over and away before being caught by the wagging tail, or the rising bottom. It wasn't for the faint-hearted, but I was willing to give it a try.

Things would have been okay if that's all I had tried. Unfortunately I also tried to take him for a walk. Getting to the Common wasn't too bad. It's just at the top of our road and usually takes a minute to reach. Harrison was eager so he shaved a bit of time off that, probably about fifty-five seconds. One moment we were standing outside my house, the next we were underneath a tree watching a squirrel disappear into its branches. I have absolutely no recollection of how we got there or of my feet ever touching the ground. Out of a sense of self-preservation, if for no other reason, I let Harrison off the lead and he took off. Before I knew what was happening, he was in the pond and making for the swans, which was the closest thing to migrating geese our pond can offer. He didn't seem to mind the difference and narrowed down the hunt to one poor swan who soon looked as if he was experiencing his life flash before his eyes. Thankfully, before the swan could find out just how soft a Chesapeake Bay retriever's mouth is, Harrison got distracted by someone nearby throwing a ball for his dog and veered off in that direction. It was hard to tell who was more relieved, me or the swan.

Harrison had a great time. He chased balls, none of which were his; he chased sticks, some of which were; and he rolled in mud puddles, making sure that not a single inch of him was left uncovered. He was large and lively and full of life and it was such fun watching him have fun.

Sadly, all good things must come to an end and it eventually came time for us to go home. Even more sadly, Harrison didn't seem to agree with that decision. We got as far as the road that separates us from the Common when he tried to run around me to get back. He pulled. I pulled back. He was winning and would have had me over if I hadn't planted my feet, bent my knees and leaned back as far as I could go. Right then, he tried another tack and simply sat down and started chewing his lead. It was a great strategy. Before long, the lead was wound so tightly around my wrist that I could hear my fingers crying. Or maybe that was me crying. I couldn't get him to stop chewing, I couldn't get him to move, I couldn't get the lead off my wrist and I really couldn't get out of the way of the oncoming car. Luckily, it's a very quiet street and the driver saw what was happening. He and a passerby both came rushing to help and before long we had the circulation going back into my hand and the dog up and reluctantly moving forward. I somehow got us home and as soon as we arrived I put down the lead and calmly, but firmly, announced, many times, that I was completely, utterly and irrevocably abdicating all responsibility for walking the dog. And I meant it. From then on, Tom and Christopher took turns and while they were better at it than I was, neither one of them made it look as easy as Melanie, the toddler and the baby did. Although Tom did proudly announce one morning that he had taught him to heel. I assumed he meant that Harrison was up on the Common grabbing people by their heels. By then, Harrison had seen his food bowl and I was too busy trying to get out of his way to ask.

Once I didn't have to walk him, Harrison was a bit easier to handle but he was still not an easy dog. Although he didn't have a mean bone in his body, he was dangerous nonetheless. His tail could knock you over, literally. It felt as if you had been hit with a tree trunk, a very big tree trunk, and if that wasn't bad enough, one of his favourite games was to grab your feet as you came down the stairs. As much as I came to like Harrison, I did start to worry a little about him living in a house with small children.

Yet despite the problems he caused, Harrison was a great dog. He was bright and friendly and had a lovely temperament. It wasn't his fault that he was just too big, too enthusiastic, too powerful and much too far away from the Chesapeake Bay. When Melanie got back from Barbados, looking too tanned and healthy and rested for a woman with two small children, I mentioned my concerns, and I think I was preaching to the converted, but her husband loved the dog and thought that everything was going to be fine. They did compromise, however, and soon afterwards Harrison got shipped off to a residential obedience school where they may not have been able to make him much smaller but they were at least able to make him a bit easier to control.

Meanwhile, a combination of the trials of Harrison's stay and the envy inspired by Melanie's Bajan tan, prompted us to start thinking about our own holiday. We have always been the kind of family who spend our limited funds on experiences and memories rather than on possessions or practicalities, which could explain why the house was slowly falling down around our ears. (Although, when you think about it, that works out fairly well if you want to be a Pet Nanny. There is, after all, very little that a dog can do to the place that hasn't been done before.) With a much-deserved break in the pet rota coming up, and with the bit of extra money that our canine friends brought in, we decided to really push the boat out, and settled on Sri Lanka.

Our friend Margot is from Colombo, so the second I booked the holiday I phoned her with the good news. Her reaction wasn't what I expected; in fact, her exact words were, 'Oh Eileen, what have you done? Don't you listen to the news?' Okay, perhaps going somewhere with a raging civil war and a newly bombed-out airport isn't everyone's idea of the perfect holiday destination, but it had made the holiday affordable, and not everyone has a background in diplomatic escapades in remote and dangerous places – Port Moresby in PNG was probably the most violent place I had ever visited. It was democratic crime, though, so anybody could be a victim – I remember at one diplomatic reception a high-ranking minister announced, 'Well, I better be getting home, before the rascals wipe me out.' No one laughed, especially not one of my colleagues. He had had his house ransacked four times in the previous twelve months and they stole all his clothes, every time, with the sole exception of a pair of prized Italian leather loafers. The last time, however, his luck ran out. Or half ran out – they took one shoe. That proved to be the last straw for him. He was standing outside his home, waving his remaining shoe and screaming 'you forgot something' until someone from the Embassy went over to calm him down.

Suffice to say, I felt fairly well-prepared for whatever Sri Lanka could throw at us. It turned out to be a wonderful adventure and we loved the country and the people. I was surprised, though, that my lasting memory wasn't of the golden Buddhas and brilliant blue skies; it was of dogs. They were everywhere, seemingly belonging to no one but all looking cared for and well-fed. After asking our guide why that was so, he looked totally bemused by the question. He had never considered it before, because the dogs were just part of the community and taken care of by everyone. Wasn't it like that everywhere?

Despite my enthusiasm for the country, I sadly concluded that Sri Lanka was not going to be a prime location for setting up a Pet Nanny business and we returned to London, well rested and ready for our next house guest. Or, in fact, not ready, because as it turned out, nothing in the world could possibly prepare you for Buster.

Buster

I've seen dogs with some very strange habits – Aristide springs to mind – but they were all positively boring compared to Buster.

Hi Eileen,

I have another rather lovely dog called Buster. He is a six-year-old smooth collie, pulls a bit on the lead but good with other dogs. Fab indoors, fits in with house rules, sleeps downstairs. Doesn't like long car journeys, will shake and pant but isn't sick!!! Let me know your thoughts.

Love,

Serena

One afternoon, there was a knock on the door and I opened it to find the oddest-looking dog I have ever seen, standing there along with his rather forlorn-looking owner. Charlotte's first words were, 'We've just come from a little dog show up on the Common and Buster didn't win "Best Looking Dog". Can you believe that?'

Ummm, well, I sort of could, not that I said that, of course. Buster was, beyond doubt, the strangest-looking dog ever created. He looked like he was put together by committee, on a Friday afternoon after lunch at the pub. He had what was probably a very normal face, until the day that he got his snout stuck in the Hoover and someone turned it on. His eyes crossed a bit, as if trying to see the tip of his nose, and his ears seemed to have come straight off one of Christian Bale's *Batman* costumes. They had lives of their own, each going off at a slightly different angle and moving to a very different beat. Personally I would have entered him in the 'One of a Kind' category but what can I say, love really is blind.

We all moved into the kitchen for a restorative cup of tea and while I commiserated with Charlotte over the lack of a rosette, Buster walked right past me and started getting ready to piddle all over my cookbooks. 'NOOOOOOOOO!' I screamed. Proving that he really was good at fitting in with house rules, he looked at me, seemed to shrug, then immediately lifted the other leg and got the refrigerator instead. That was better. I was almost certain I could hear the sofa in the other room give a sigh of relief.

When Buster arrived a few days later to stay with us, I began to suspect that his failure at the dog show may have weighed more heavily upon him than I had previously suspected. For one thing, he didn't want to play. No amount of ball throwing or floor wrestling or tug of warring interested him. Instead he spent most of his time lying in front of the sitting room mirror, staring at himself. He didn't seem to like what he saw, judging from the expression on his face. I hoped his mood was fallout from the dog show and not because he could read minds. I would have felt bad if I had upset him with that Christian Bale remark.

When not staring at his reflection, Buster either ate the post or else lay in the hallway snapping at imaginary flies. You would be in the kitchen, or the bedroom, or the sitting room, or just about anywhere else in the house for that matter and hear …

snap … snap … snap. He could keep it up for hours. In fact, he did keep it up for hours. It was a bit unnerving but it must have worked because I haven't seen a fly in here since.

The only thing that could really make him stop staring and snapping was walking, so we started spending more and more time up on the Common. He seemed almost happy up there, although I wasn't completely convinced that he understood this whole concept of being a dog. He would eagerly run up to other dogs, but then stand there not knowing what to do next. He chased after sticks, but then just looked at them before walking away. He would let you pet him, but he didn't particularly care if you did or if you didn't. He was exceptionally good at coming when called but would then look at you as if to say, 'Yeah? What?' But what I found hardest to understand was that he could have taken me or left me, no matter how much I walked him or petted him or fed him. I was used to dogs liking me. I was actually used to dogs loving me. What was I doing wrong? I did, however, notice that he seemed to like my neighbour. That hurt.

In an effort to win his affections, I decided to take him for a long walk one day, on a different common for a change. I really didn't feel that either one of us wanted to go through his shaking and panting, but hopefully not being sick, car routine and so I packed a bag of treats for the both of us and headed off to the train station. Buster seemed pretty excited by the whole adventure. He sat on the platform, he waited patiently, he wagged his tail every now and again and he seemed to really appreciate it when I read out interesting bits from the *Metro* to him.

This happy state was not to last. From the very second the doors closed, Buster started to howl. Not your timid, tentative howl either. No, this was your throw back your head, open your mouth and really let loose type of howl. The rest of the people in the carriage didn't know what had hit them. There was no escape and there was absolutely no way to make him stop. Petting didn't work. Telling him he was a bad dog didn't work. Telling him he was a good dog didn't work. Showing him the treats, both his and mine, didn't work. Begging didn't work. Even trying to pretend that I was not standing there with an odd-looking, howling dog didn't work. Luckily for me this is England, so no one actually said anything. They all just shook their heads disapprovingly and gave me the stare that is normally reserved for the parents of crying babies on long-haul flights. Realising that I was beaten, we got off at the next stop and walked home. He seemed to like that. When we neared the house a woman I had never seen before walked up to us and said, 'Oh, that's Buster. He's such a funny dog. Have you ever heard him on a train? He's unbelievable.' Actually, I had, and he was. The real question was – why couldn't we have met her on the way *to* the station?

She wasn't the only person to stop to talk to me about Buster. In fact, it was a rare walk when someone didn't come up to me to tell me how unusual my dog was. Everyone seemed to have something to say, and not many people were too shy to say it. Most of the conversations started with 'He's a very odd-looking dog' but, if they lasted any time at all, would inevitably end with, 'but he's really sweet.'

At the end of the week Charlotte returned and I have to say, she looked like a completely different woman, ten years younger and a zillion times happier. It just shows you how restorative a good holiday can be. Or perhaps it proved that it was easier to sleep when there wasn't a dog downstairs snapping at flies. Her first words, however, on seeing Buster were to tell him how fat he was, which was a bit harsh when you consider all that snapping and walking he had been doing. If I were a psychiatrist instead of a Pet Nanny, I might be tempted to think that I had just discovered what lay at the root of his problems – always having to live up to his owner's rather high expectations. But I'm not, so I don't.

As I watched them drive away, I thought that Buster may not have been pretty enough, or apparently thin enough, as Charlotte may have liked, but there was no doubt that she loved him. Who wouldn't? He is a completely, totally and utterly unique individual and it was surprisingly good fun watching him to see what he would do next. In a world of perfect, identical models, Buster is that wonderful thing, a true original.

Coco and Alaska

If you were looking for identical models, you need look no further than Coco and Alaska. They looked so much alike that we gave up trying to figure out who was who and wound up calling them both Cocaska.

Hi Eileen,

I've got two little West Highland terriers, Coco (6) and Alaska (4), aunt and niece, I think. They are very affectionate, don't yap, friendly with other dogs and children. Love feet!! What do you think?

Sx

I don't know why but I always thought that West Highland terriers were those sour-faced, brownish-coloured dogs who look a bit like the school janitor in *The Simpsons,* so it was a wonderful surprise when I opened the door one morning to find two completely identical and ridiculously cute little dogs sitting on my doormat. They were obviously models, probably for those black velvet paintings that no one ever seems to buy but are always in a certain kind of gift shop.

Their owner, Sally, was little and cute herself. She is the sort of woman who can wear a raincoat with style and, I couldn't help but notice, the tiniest high heels I have ever seen that were not actually made of plastic and attached to a Barbie doll. The entire encounter brought to mind the diplomatic career that I had left behind. Before I met Tom, I had imagined travelling the world with a terrier-type dog named Fifi and gracing diplomatic receptions in outfits which put Sally to shame. Instead, I was wearing wellies and fast becoming the Dog Woman of Wandsworth. Only briefly did I consider the logic of my past decisions – looking at the latest pair of candidates before me, I knew I'd made the right choice.

Sally works every now and again for a mega lawyer and she needed someone to watch 'the girls' while she was in the office. It seemed like a lot of effort for her to drop them off and pick them up every day and I told her that I would be happy to have them overnight if that made things easier for her. But she didn't like that idea at all. Her husband travels a lot and her only child, Georgia, is away at boarding school, so the girls are her companions and she didn't want to be parted from them any longer than necessary. I could soon see why. They loved her. The entire time we sat on the sofas drinking our tea, Coco and Alaska lay with their heads on her lap and took it in turns to look up at her adoringly. Either that or they were wondering if I was ever planning on painting the ceiling. I frequently wonder the same thing myself.

Anyway, we decided that the girls would, if not love at least tolerate, hanging out with a less stylish crowd for a few weeks and it was settled that they would come to us first thing on the following Monday morning. The day arrived and so did Sally, with her two little companions, who stood there looking adorable while Sally handed over their bowls and pre-measured dinners and leads and treats and toys and everything else they might need before she saw them again. She wanted to know if

I had any questions before she left and I had to admit that I did – I wanted to know which dog was which. I honestly could not tell them apart. She seemed a bit taken aback by this because, apparently, Alaska has a slightly wider smile than her niece (or was it aunt?), whereas Coco's coat is a shade darker (or was that lighter?). When I told her that neither of those two tips was particularly helpful, she said, 'Oh, well Coco's collar is claret and Alaska's is purple.' Claret? Is that a colour? Apparently so; it's a shade of purple. So that was helpful. After a lengthy farewell, Sally went off into the world of billion-pound deals while Coco and Alaska made themselves at home and I tried to figure out why they didn't have their names on their collars.

After spending about half an hour with the girls, I seriously started wondering why Sally couldn't just take them into work with her and leave them in her bottom desk drawer. They were the quietest, calmest dogs I had ever met. They loved sitting on your lap, or sleeping at your feet, or simply staring at you. It wouldn't have surprised me at all to discover that they were really battery-operated, with no batteries.

At least I would have believed that if I hadn't made the mistake of trying to go upstairs. That's when they sprang into life. Those two dogs were fiends for feet. But not just any old feet. They liked feet when combined with stairs. They just darted in and out, made little attacks and then backed away. They were relentless and telling them to stop made no impression on them at all. You could try running up and down, but they could always go faster. You could try sitting down on the steps and waiting until they got bored and went away, but they never did. They knew that at some point you had to go either up or down and they were going to be there when it happened. It made you realise how the Spanish Armada must have felt when those pesky little English ships attacked, and we all know what happened to the Spanish Armada. You had to be careful because your life was in serious danger, especially if you were foolish enough to be carrying anything that obscured your vision. I could just imagine someone coming home and finding me lying in a heap at the bottom of the stairs, surrounded by the laundry and with two sweet little dogs lying next to me looking utterly adorable.

The only thing they enjoyed nearly as much as feet was their dinner. They ate something which had to be ordered from a speciality shop in north London and which involved reindeers and oats, or was that Highland cattle and thistles? I'm not sure, but it was gaspingly expensive, came in a very pretty bag and was served in bowls that looked like miniature woks. I've seen a few dog bowls in my time, but nothing like these. I absolutely loved them. They were stylish and fun and, of course, totally identical. Just like the girls.

Babs

The girls were adorable, but then there came another dog who rather unexpectedly wormed her way into a very tall boy's heart.

Hi Eileen,

Babs is a miniature dachshund. She will be only about ten weeks old but I think she will have had her jabs so should be okay. Obviously she won't need much in the way of walking but I don't have any more info as Caroline doesn't even pick her up until the weekend. Perhaps we should introduce you early next week and see what you think.

Regards,

Sx

The reason I am telling you about Babs isn't because she was a cute dachshund puppy, or because she liked sitting in the fruit bowl, or because she kept trying to make friends with that little dog she saw in the mirror, or even because her owner had attended the same university as Kimberly and so gave me hope that there were paying jobs after Edinburgh. No, the reason I am telling you about Babs is because she was my nephew Doug's favourite dog, which is something that I still find hard to believe.

Doug is enormously tall, very athletic, with a wide smile and an engaging manner. Oh, and he's also extremely good-looking. He must have been around twenty years old at the time and was staying with us for the summer, as my niece Mary Kate had done the previous year. I love it when our extended family come to stay – we don't have many relatives in this country so it's a real treat when they're here. It's wonderful being able to use the words 'niece' and 'nephew', introducing them to the neighbourhood and seeing my children spend time with their cousins. Perhaps that is why I had taken to the life of a Pet Nanny so keenly – although the vast majority of our family is elsewhere, the dogs gave us a chance to put down real roots in our community. Through them we were getting an ever-increasing circle of friends and acquaintances, and it made me feel like I belonged there, the way I felt growing up in Astoria.

Doug, being from Tom's side of the family, wasn't from urban New York but rather from a beautiful, tidy, well-organised home in Virginia, where things were picked up when they were dropped, fixed when they broke and ironed when they were washed. He arrived in London to find himself in a wildly chaotic household where nothing was as you would expect it to be and where you couldn't move without tripping over a dog. Doug doesn't come from a family of pet owners and he wasn't used to the mayhem that can result from having a few extra beasties around the place, especially at mealtimes. Happily he adapted to his new environment fairly well and even managed to routinely turn negatives into positives. The fact, for example, that we were eating dinner at 11pm one night was apparently because we did not let rigid rules like dinnertime control our lives. That made me feel better about the fact that I regularly fed him in almost total darkness.

Doug also pitched in and did his bit with the dogs. He walked the Labradors, fed the Tibetan terriers, threw balls for the retrievers, went jogging with the salukis, hauled the Portuguese water dogs out of the pond and dutifully petted whoever happened to be around him at the time. But I don't think he ever really connected with any of them until Babs the Wonder Dog came into his life.

Babs, a miniature dachshund, was only a few weeks old and a few pounds heavy. She could literally fit into Doug's cupped hands, and the fact that, as it turned out, she hadn't had all her shots and couldn't be put on the ground outside the house never mattered because from the moment she arrived she went everywhere in Doug's pocket. He habitually wore one of those sweatshirts with the pouch in front where you can keep your hands warm and it quickly became Babs's favourite place. She would go in one way, curl around in the middle and go to sleep. Or else she would stick her nose out one end and watch the world go by, from a great height. When I think about it, she was a pretty brave little dog. Either that or she just didn't notice that she was much higher up than a puppy should be. I still have a vivid memory of standing next to Doug as he reached up to fix a curtain rail and finding myself eyeball to eyeball with Babs. I blinked first.

One day, seeing the two of them together, I asked Doug why a sporty guy like him wouldn't rather be up on the Common playing Frisbee with a large, fast dog instead of playing mother kangaroo to a bundle of fluff and he gave me his big, slow smile and said, 'I don't know Auntie Eileen. I guess it's just because I kinda like her.'

We'll make a dog owner out of him yet.

Harvey

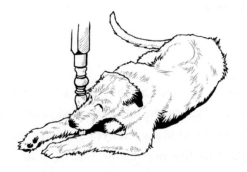

Some dogs need more room than a mere 175-acre common can provide and more attention than can be given in only twenty-four hours a day. Which could explain why not all my Pet Nanny experiences work out well. For example … Harvey.

Hi Eileen,

I've got Harvey, a year-old Irish wolfhound. He is a beautiful boy who likes long walks, lots of space and your undivided attention. His family lives near you and are going on holiday for two weeks. Why don't you meet and see what you think? Let me know.

Regards,

Serena x

Well, I met Harvey and straight away I thought the dog was totally insane. He was the size of a small pony, had enough energy to keep London alight for years and was out of control. Within the first five minutes he was here, he completely destroyed a football that he had found in the garden and then punctured Christopher's favourite rugby ball – although in fairness to him, at least he didn't eat it. His owner, a very nice woman named Fiona, and I chased him around the garden for what seemed like hours trying to get him to drop it, to no avail. Apparently he is kept on a lead in his own garden because he eats the plants. He needs to be watched constantly inside the house because he chews anything, including the kitchen cabinets. He sleeps in a bare basket because he has destroyed nine cushions in six months (or possibly weeks or even days) and his family has given up. He isn't welcome at her sister's house any more because he ate the table leg. And you have to be careful with him on the Common because he runs off with people's balls/shoes/picnics. Honestly, he was here for ten minutes and I needed a little lie down when they left. I told Tom about him and he said, 'Absolutely not', which I have to admit was a pretty good decision.

Kimberly, who was home for the week, laughed when I said that I wasn't having Harvey. Apparently she thought that I would never say no to anyone, other than her of course. If it had been up to her, there would have been quite a few other dogs on the 'no' list. Every one, in fact, who had ever ventured into her bedroom, which I have to admit is quite a few of them. I don't think she would mind if they just wandered in, sniffed around and wandered out again, but they all seemed to love chewing on her possessions. They didn't care what it was, they weren't picky, as long as it was in reach it was acceptable. And since everything she owned was on the floor, that was every-thing. We had come to an agreement that I would reimburse her for anything that got destroyed but I soon started suspect-ing that she was using the situation as a way of saying 'out with the old and in with the new'. Since I told her to close her door or accept the consequences, things have quietened down, a bit.

I felt bad about saying no to Harvey, who was the first and only dog that I have ever rejected. But to be honest, Fiona didn't help. She spent the entire time she was here telling me in glorious detail about all of his misdeeds. By the time they left, I was convinced that the dog needed a tranquillizer dart. Apparently, though, he was only so hyper because he hadn't had his two (2) hour morning walk yet. That, it turned out, is followed by a two (2) hour afternoon walk and a 'short' one (1) hour evening walk.

Should we have let him come? Perhaps if we were willing to spend the next two weeks on the Common he would have calmed down, not eaten the plants or the furniture and not driven us crazy, but if he didn't I couldn't honestly say that I hadn't been warned.

To be fair, Harvey was a pretty nice dog. It wasn't his fault that he was enormous and lived in a terraced house in London. Perhaps there should be a law that certain kinds of dogs shouldn't live in certain postcodes, or maybe we could have one of those height charts you see at fairs that says, 'You have to be this high …' but instead of a clown saying you can't get on the ride if you are too small, it could be a cut-out of a friendly-looking hound holding his paw out and saying you can't live in the house if you are too big.

Of course, as Sod's law would have it, Harvey and his family only live around the corner from us and I see them several times every day walking him to and from the Common. I can't say that they look particularly friendly. Perhaps they're just tired, of either walking so much or of living in a house with no furniture.

Jessie

I thought Harvey was bad, but that was only because I had yet to meet Jessie.

Hi Eileen,

I've got a wonderful eleven-month-old wheaten terrier called Jessie. She is fully trained, doesn't chew, sleeps downstairs in her crate, not a barker, doesn't swim so is safe near the pond. In fact, she is very chilled, loves children, other dogs and company. What do you think?

Love,

Sx

With hindsight, what I should have thought was … RUN! But at the time I thought that she sounded nice, and so did her owner Debbie. She had grown up with dogs and had been around them all her life and now she wanted her children to have the same experience. Of course, I later learned that she had grown up in a huge house in the country where all her dogs had lots of room to roam and to get into their mischief outside. But that knowledge came too late.

On a lovely summer day Jessie the wheaten terrier arrived, complete with a large crate and an even larger assortment of toys. She also came with a list of instructions. For a start, she was absolutely not allowed upstairs, which was a bit of a problem since the days of stair gates were long behind us. Still, with a bit of ingenuity and a fervent prayer that there would not be a fire in the middle of the night that required us to use the staircase as an escape route, we managed to set up a fairly efficient blockade.

She was also supposed to sleep in her crate, but with the door open. I wasn't sure what the point of that was, but perhaps it was Jessie's personal space and she liked seeing the world through bars. So we set her crate up, kept the door opened and filled it with her toys. It did actually look very cosy.

After a very pleasant first day together, during which she explored the Common, the garden and the rubbish, we said goodnight to her, put her in her open crate and went upstairs, having first successfully negotiated the barrier of assorted discarded furniture parts. I must admit that I was pretty pleased with my efforts. I hadn't seen a barricade that impressive since the time we went to see *Les Misérables*.

The next morning I came downstairs, surprised by how remarkably quiet Jessie had been during the night – which turned out to have been very remarkable indeed when you consider what she had been up to. The first thing I noticed was how cute she looked, lying there fast asleep. The second was that she was lying on the remains of her bedding. I reluctantly tore my eyes away from her and started looking around the room and soon realised why she was still sleeping. She must have been completely exhausted by the hard work of staying up all night and chewing everything in sight. The entire ground floor was like a scene out of *Jaws*, but without the boat. Most things didn't matter – it really was time for that wicker table to go anyway, and Christopher's shoes would have needed replacing eventually. But tragically, she also got Tom's grand-parents' Chinese rug, the one they received as a present when they were based in China in the 1920s. She didn't eat the whole rug (it was after all very large and the night was only so long), but she made good inroads into it and got one entire corner and a good part of one side. I thought that perhaps I could hide it from him until I got it repaired, but there really is only so much strategic positioning of furniture that you can achieve.

While I went to make a nice cup of tea, Tom, a man who loves dogs, sat staring at his rug, trying not to cry, and contemplating whether to murder Jessie or her owners. He eventually decided on the owners who were, after all, the people who said that she didn't chew, and to leave the crate door open so she could come and go as she wanted and to barricade the stairs so she couldn't go upstairs, which basically left her free to roam all night at will.

After the rug incident I felt it was best to have her in sight at all times, so the barricade came down and the crate got locked at night, but the damage was done. Her owners picked her up a few days later and when told what had happened said, 'Oh dear', or words to that effect. They seemed surprised that she had chewed anything (everything). Perhaps she doesn't do that at home, or perhaps they haven't noticed.

We eventually got a quote in from a nice man who was very complimentary about 95 per cent of our antique, Chinese silk rug. The missing 5 per cent of it was going to cost £2,525 to repair. Jessie's owners had very little to say about that, not even 'sorry', which would have been a very good start. We never saw Jessie again, which was a shame because she was a nice dog – it's not a puppy's fault that she is a puppy. But her stay was probably the one that most made me question whether or not to continue as a Pet Nanny. The house was really taking a beating. Not only were the sofas developing distinctive dog-shaped depressions, but the carpets were beginning to resemble a connect-the-dots puzzle. One of the biggest downsides of having non-stop dogs, especially in a climate like this, is the mud. And that's just what Tom tracks in. He's less responsible for all the dog hairs. The result was that some days the entrance hall looked like Flanders in 1915, while on others it resembled an Old Western town with fur filling in for drifting tumbleweeds. Something had to change and so, after a bit of lateral thinking, we took up the carpet, polished up the floorboards and invested in a top-of-the-range mop. That diplomatic problem-solving training came in handy again.

Meanwhile I had also gradually realised that while it was good to put people's minds at ease so they could go off and enjoy their holidays, a Pet Nanny was also there when someone's mother died unexpectedly and they had to rush off to the other end of the country, or they became too ill to watch their dog for a few days or had an emergency at work. As time went on, I became increasingly aware that I was helping to provide a vital service. Okay, I wasn't brokering peace in the Middle East or helping to channel American aid to Africa but I was doing something worthwhile. And that felt like a very good thing indeed and worth persevering, despite the occasional bad experience.

Plus it was keeping me fit.

Roux and Simon

Jessie may not have had a return visit, but some of our visitors are so lovely, we're happy to have them over and over again.

Hi Eileen,

I've got two little Texan dachshunds! Roux, nine, black and tan, friendly, loves treats, does tricks. Simon, about seven, red, rescue dog, timid. Both greedy, neither likes going out in the rain. Do you want to meet them?

Love,

Sx

It's hard to remember a time when we didn't know Simon and Roux, or their owners. Jason and Lisa are a lovely young couple who are over here from Texas for a few years. She's an accountant and he's a cardiac physiotherapist. Neither one looks old enough to be anything other than students, but there you go. Neither one, I suspect, is completely aware of the fact that Simon and Roux are dogs.

Roux, in the days when he was an only dog, was the ring bearer at their wedding. They devised a contraption that was strapped around his middle to which the rings were attached. I'm not entirely clear about this but it sounded a bit like those boxes that tiger hunters used to put atop elephants during the Raj, except with Velcro. I'm also not sure if someone led him down the aisle or if he managed it under his own steam but, knowing him the way I do, I suspect they had a small boy walking in front of him, dangling bits of food.

Although he was not much more than ankle-high, Roux was very brave and adventurous, and loved exploring new places, especially if those places hold, or once held, food. He absolutely loved scavenging. It was his favourite hobby. In fact, one of the first things you had to learn when watching him was to guard the rubbish. No matter how careful you thought you had been, it was always best to check again. If you left even a slight chink in your defences, you would come downstairs in the morning to find the remains of last night's dinner strewn across the entire kitchen floor. He was like Houdini, except that he escaped into, not out of, and there were no chains involved, and he was a dog. Though I bet Houdini wasn't nearly as good at tricks. Roux's best one involved him sitting down (on a nice, soft carpet; he didn't do it if the floor was too cold or hard), having someone pretend to hold a gun to his head and say, 'Bang', after which he immediately fell down. I know, it was a bit odd but you have to remember that Roux was from Texas.

Simon, meanwhile, was a very timid boy. But then, he had a very traumatic childhood. He was found floating alone in the flood waters after Hurricane Katrina hit the southern US coast in 2005. His picture went up on websites and into newspapers but no one claimed him and he was eventually put up for adoption. That's when his luck took a turn for the better because Jason and Lisa saw him, fell in love with him and made him the fourth member of the family. Soon afterwards, he was on his way to Europe. I often wonder what his original owners would say if they knew. I'm sure that when they wondered about what happened to him, the idea that he was living happily in London was never one of their options.

Simon was also greedy, but in a different way from Roux. Whereas Roux loved food, Simon shovelled it down in a frenzy, as if he didn't know where his next meal was coming from and was afraid that someone was going to take the current one away from him. He was also needier and more vulnerable than his brother – he had a way of making you want to take care of him. Even Kimberly felt that way. His favourite thing in the world was to snuggle down with you, especially if you happened to be under a duvet at the time. If not, he improvised and was willing to just stick his head under your jumper while the rest of him hung out. He was also an enormous football fan, American that is, and loved staying up late with Christopher to watch games on television. The only bone of contention between them was that Christopher supports the New York Giants while Simon roots for the Dallas Cowboys. Guess you can't blame him really, he picked up that bad habit from Jason.

We see a lot of the boys, and through their owners we hear a lot about the world. Jason calls us from wherever he is, several times, just to see how they are doing. He can't help himself. He knows that I have had dogs since before he was born but he worries. He worries about Simon's tummy and Roux's back, about Simon getting on with the other dogs, and Roux getting into the rubbish. He worries about whether the boys are eating, if they are behaving themselves, if it's raining too much for them to go out for walks, and if Roux is feeling neglected because everyone fusses so much over Simon and, and, and. It's rather endearing but does make you worry for any future children he may have. I used to send him nightly emails with photos of the boys' day, but then I realised that I rather enjoyed the phone calls. It was fun to see where they would come from next.

He has called us from Spain, where he was running the bulls; Nigeria, where he was attending a chieftain's enthronement ceremony; Turkey, where he was in a mud bath; and from Las Vegas, where he was at a stag party – making him probably the only person in the history of stag parties to step outside for a few minutes to phone another continent to check on the dogs. My favourite, however, was the time he called from India, where he was visiting the Taj Mahal. By strange coincidence, fifteen minutes earlier I had received a call from a backpacking Kimberly, also at the Taj Mahal, who was phoning to tell me that it was the most romantic and wonderful place in the world. When Jason phoned, it was to ask if Roux's cough was any better. I suppose that's the difference between men and women. I told Jason that I was tired of getting phone calls from a famous bench in India, that the boys were fine and to go find my daughter.

Part of the boys' attraction for me and Tom was undoubt-edly their owners, people we would never have met if it weren't for the dogs. They were such an appealing young couple, fellow Americans a long way from home, exploring the universe and enjoying every second of it. It was exciting to see the world through their eyes, eyes which not that long ago had been our own. To hear their stories of where they had been, what they had seen and done and thought about, was to recapture a bit of the wonder of our own earlier experiences. Not that we ever told them that; why ruin their magic of having been the first to discover it all? It brought back the memories of my diplomatic years: the thrill of living in far-flung places, of walking through the jungle with an astronaut or helping a champion boxer plan a trip to Africa – Muhammad Ali, since you asked. I had been working at the African Bureau at the time, where my main job was to get people to do things that they didn't want to do, much faster than they intended to do them. In the few days that Ali was in the office, I became immensely popular – suddenly no one was too busy to do anything I wanted, and people were constantly popping in to have a word about things with the vaguest connection to Africa. I think I met almost everyone who worked in the State Department, and a few who didn't. Those were the days where I was at the centre of important things, and Jason and Lisa reminded me what that was like.

Not that I miss it – my life has moved on, and now I'm just as happy to stay at home in the company of a pair of wonderfully entertaining Texan dachshunds, while their owners jet off around the world. Particularly at Christmas time. Another thing we loved about the boys was that we were lucky enough to have them for Christmas every year. Jason and Lisa always spent the holidays with their families in the USA, and so the boys spent them with us. They have their own little stockings and holiday hats and are in every family Christmas photo taken over the past few years. Sadly for us, Simon and Roux were always destined to return home and have recently gone back to Texas for good. I don't know how we are going to manage Christmas without them. It really doesn't bear thinking about. So I don't.

Ruby

Simon and Roux may have been from Texas, but Ruby was from really far away. Actually she was from only two streets away, but her ancestors were a different story altogether.

Hi Eileen,

I have a four-year-old Lhasa apso called Ruby. She's very easy, but rather dull and not allowed off the lead. She's fine with children as long as they don't want to play with her, but dislikes postmen and vacuum cleaners. Would you be up for it?

Love,

Serena

A Lhasa apso? I thought they were those strange-looking, long-necked creatures who carried people around Peru, which seemed a bit unusual but not totally beyond the realm of possibility, given the neighbourhood we live in. But no, after a quick trip to Wikipedia, I discovered that they were merely 'small dogs originating in Tibet who were bred as interior sentinels in Buddhist monasteries to alert the monks to intruders'. Of course they are. No wonder Serena described Ruby as dull.

The children were at the stage where they didn't get up before noon and wouldn't speak, much less play with, small dogs for many hours after that. And I was at the stage where I had realised the total futility of hoovering in a canine-filled household. As for the postman, he had long since given up on the idea of trying to put things through the letter box. Instead, and who could really blame him, he had adopted a new method of delivery; he simply placed them on the mat, rang the bell and sprinted, Usain Bolt-like, back down the path. Having considered all those things, I decided that I was up for it and invited the Tibetan sentinel and her owner around for tea.

Ruby and Jez, who I assumed was her owner, duly turned up a few days later. Ruby was small, sweet, fluffy and wearing a pink bow to keep the fur out of her eyes. It was hard to imagine she would worry anyone intrepid enough to break into a Tibetan monastery, but that was before I heard her 'sonorous, bell-like voice'. She may have weighed less than a bag of potatoes but it was all bark and if the sound that came out of her was either 'sonorous' or 'bell-like', then I had just discovered yet another reason to be glad that I was not a Tibetan monk.

Jez, meanwhile, was not small, sweet or fluffy. Or sonorous or bell-like, come to think of it. And he certainly didn't have a pink bow. He was a very nice-looking young man but quite dour. Perhaps he was a little embarrassed to be seen in daylight in the company of a small dog with a pink bow or perhaps it was because, as he mentioned several times, Ruby wasn't really his dog but rather his sister's and just happened to live in the same house as him. Either way, he could have been a contender for most depressing human being in the universe. Over the course of the next half hour, I discovered that: he and his family were thinking of moving to Somerset (sigh); his favourite team was Chelsea (sigh); he and his parents were going on holiday to Tuscany (sigh); that it was best to keep the dog on the lead (sigh); that she tried to sneak upstairs at night (sigh); and that she preferred human food to dog food (really big sigh). In reaction, I got more maniacally upbeat and enthusiastic by the second and could hear myself turning into Bertie Wooster's more optimistic sister. By the end I wasn't sure which one of us was coming off as stranger. It made you feel sorry for poor Ruby, who by this time must have been seriously wishing that she was back in Tibet.

On the appointed day Ruby arrived, we went for a walk up on the Common and by the time we came back I was totally in love with her. She had an amazing way of looking at the world that was so utterly superior and dismissive that you just had to laugh, not to mention a walk that would make a supermodel turn green with envy. A lot of people might have described her as boring, which was an opinion that I could understand if you didn't know her because she really didn't do much. But it was the way that she did it, or more accurately didn't do it, that made her so brilliant. The dog had style.

She also had a fan. Tom was smitten with her and became very smug because, unusually for one of our charges, Ruby preferred lying on his tummy to mine. He thought it was because she liked him more than she did me, whereas I knew that it was simply because she liked waterbeds rather than hard, flat surfaces. Still, I never told him that. Everyone needs their little delusions.

I used to take Ruby into the office with me quite a bit. Our office at the time was a short walk from home, in a converted Victorian stable with worn granite stairs, sloping roofs and windows that you had to nail shut in winter so they didn't slide open. It also had a kitchen sink where you could have either cold water or hot water but never both at the same time. It had character and a sense of history and it suited us perfectly, especially since the dogs were always welcome. Although on this occasion I hadn't actually planned on taking Ruby in. I had just dropped in to pick something up, with her in tow, and while we were in there we bumped into Ratika. It was hard to get Ruby home again after that. Ratika was working part-time and had just arrived from India to attend university here. She was very homesick and especially missed her own little Lhasa apso. So Ruby would go in to get petted and hugged and chatted to and they were both very happy with the arrangement. Unfortunately another part-time student was a very strict Muslim and, I hadn't known this before, Muslims consider dogs unclean and can't touch them or have anything to do with them. Tom started to notice that the entire office had begun revolving around Ruby – both pro and anti factions – and that not much work was getting done. So we eventually compromised. Ruby would come in only on the days when Mustafa wasn't there and Ratika would drop by the house to take her out for walks on the days when he was.

We saw Ruby a lot over the next few months as her family went to California to see Jez's brother (sigh), to Norway to see his mother's sister (sigh) and to France just for the heck of it (sigh), not to mention when they had the basement dug out and turned into a home cinema (sigh – yes, honestly). Still, their loss was our gain and it got harder and harder to hand her back. Sadly for us, though, she and her family eventually moved to Somerset. Now that really was a reason to sigh.

Jackson

There was no sighing when it came to Jackson. He was a dog who really enjoyed life, in several languages.

Hi Eileen,
I have a two-year-old black flat coat retriever, named Jackson. He loves ponds, doesn't chew (furniture, shoes, post, tissues, socks), and likes other dogs and children once he has smelled them. He is a lovely dog, but large!! Will you meet him?
Love,
Sx

I have to admit that the real reason I wanted to meet Jackson was because his description was so wonderful. A dog who liked children once he had smelled them? A dog who wouldn't chew a specific list of things, but presumably everything else in the universe? A dog who liked ponds? A dog named Jackson? Who would not want to meet him?

I wasn't disappointed. Jackson was, as advertised, a lovely, large dog. He even looked large when he stood next to his owner, Arni, who was a Viking of a man. I'm not exaggerating, he really was. Arni, all six feet six inches of him, was from Greenland and arrived one evening in a white, cable-knit fisherman's jumper, blonde hair blowing in the wind, with an enormous black dog at his side. For a moment I thought that I had stumbled into an ad for whisky or aftershave, or some other manly product, until I realised that they were standing in my doorway, and that Vikings don't normally wear fishermen's jumpers or arrive in Volvos.

When I finally stopped staring at Arni and his dog, I noticed that there was a very small, dark boy standing behind them. He was introduced as Miquel, Arni's son. He was a sweet little boy, a bit on the shy side or possibly just frightened of being stepped on by either his father or his dog. Arni, I learned, was a diplomat and the family had just arrived in London from Venezuela. I also learned that Miquel's younger brother had named the dog Jackson, on the grounds that Jackson was a good name for a dog. It's hard to argue with that.

Jackson had obviously already smelled Miquel because they got along very well and the two of them sat on the floor, playing with a rather strange-looking, lopsided ball that Miquel had taken out of his pocket. I was torn between watching Arni drinking tea out of what I had previously regarded as a normal-sized mug and watching Jackson to see if he chewed the ball, which was, after all, not on the list of non-chewable items. Both mug and ball survived their respective encounters and it was soon decided that Jackson would like to come back to stay with us.

Before he left, Arni handed me a list of things that I ought to know about Jackson. Apparently he loved jumping into ponds and had to be prevented from doing so because of a tendency towards ear infections. He liked to leave balls at the bottom of staircases, so you had to be careful first thing in the morning. He loved fish of any sort, but especially sardines. There was also a list of words that he understood: sit, no, stop, good dog, eat, come, out. But sadly, he only understood them in Greenlandic and Spanish because 'his English isn't that good yet'. Luckily Arni also supplied the translations.

Jackson arrived a few days later and didn't seem to let his lack of English stand in the way of having a good time. He developed his own little routines. First thing every morning he had to go out and patrol the back garden to make sure that no wildlife had invaded during the night. At least that's what I think he was doing. Those Vikings are vigilant sorts, after all. Then he would run upstairs to see if Christopher was awake and available for playing with. He never seemed deterred by the fact that in the entire time he was with us, Christopher was never once awake, at least not before he jumped on him. Still, Christopher – a boy who it must be said is not at his absolute best in the morning – seemed strangely okay with getting woken up by Jackson. He thought he was a great dog. Not in small part, I suspect, because his rugby team had won by an unprecedented 22–0 the time Jackson had come to watch them play. He instantly became the boys' good luck charm and there was even talk of getting him a team shirt.

Cultural differences popped up a lot during Jackson's stay. For starters, he never seemed to know which way to look when crossing the road. Unfortunately, Arni had omitted 'left' and 'right' from my list, so I had to resort to pointing. It didn't work. Jackson could not be made to look where I was pointing, no matter how much I flapped my arms about and tried to turn his head and shouted, 'No not this way, the other way.' A taxi slowed down once but thought better of it after either catching sight of the size of Jackson or the mad look in my eye, and sped off without stopping. Thinking back on it, I'm not sure why the driver thought I needed a taxi. I could have just ridden the dog wherever I wanted to go, once we overcame our problems with directions.

Another thing that Jackson could not get the hang of was bathtubs. Perhaps he had never seen one before. Perhaps they use only showers or saunas in Greenland. Or, more likely, perhaps he only understood the sentence 'Stay downstairs, I'm going to have a bath' in one of his mother tongues. Whatever the reason, he wandered in one day while I was having a bath and, without pausing for a second, started trying to climb in. He got both paws and most of his chest in before he realised that something was not right. The look on his face when he discovered that he was getting wet was brilliant. He simply couldn't understand how that had happened. I tried remembering the Greenlandic for 'out' but I was laughing so hard that I couldn't, so I settled for saying it very loudly in English. It seemed to work although I got the feeling, as he shook his head and headed out the door, that Jackson wasn't too impressed with either my linguistic skills or my tub.

I do know, however, that having Jackson stay with us was a real pleasure. He was a large, lovely, trilingual dog and everything in the world seemed to surprise and delight him. He would look at something and then turn his head to you in such a way that you just knew he was thinking, 'Did you see THAT?!'

I learned a lot from Jackson's visit, besides what the capital of Greenland is (Nuuk, I knew you were curious). I also discovered that: it isn't easy preventing an enormous dog who wants to go into a pond from doing so, no matter how many languages you yell 'stop' at him in; while large dogs might like smelling small children, it's not always well-received by said infants; it's hard to spot balls at the bottom of the staircase even if it isn't first thing in the morning; and the Greenlandic words for 'good dog' are almost impossible to pronounce, although that didn't really matter because Jackson seemed to get the message anyway.

Barney and Maxwell

Just like the Special Relationship between the USA and Britain, some longstanding partnerships are meant to be. Barney and Maxwell are a perfect pair.

Hi Eileen,

Gosh, will it ever end? I now have Maxwell, female (!?!?!), Lakeland terrier, seven, and Barney, male, Alsatian/boxer cross, fourteen months. Barney may pull on the lead if excited, neither fights, though apparently Maxwell will have a go at Barney if he bothers her too much to play! Barney is very obedient, Maxwell, typical terrier, will come when she's ready but particularly if you have a treat. Not huge walks, Barney has hip displacia (spelling?!) so between half to an hour per day. Barney is puppy-like, very soft and thinks he's a small dog. Very licky. Maxwell is not overly affectionate but they both like company.

Love,

Sx

Most people who have more than one dog tend to stick with the same breed. And so you get two dachshunds or two Labs or two Westies. Or they at least have vaguely similar dogs, such as a wheaten and a bearded terrier. Not so Nick and Robin. They have the largest, soppiest dog I have ever met, along with one of the smallest and most reserved. Come to think of it, Nick and Robin are a little mismatched themselves. Where Nick is tall, fair, a director of travelogues and television commercials and thus artistic, Robin is small, dark, a policeman and so practical. But they are both great guys and we always enjoy catching up with them when they come to drop off or collect their dogs.

That is one of the wonderful and unexpected benefits of being a Pet Nanny – the opportunity to meet a wide circle of people and learn first-hand information about things you might never otherwise encounter. Frequently, while the dogs were running around the garden, we've been inside drinking tea and pumping Nick and Robin for information. We had a new career-related question or two for them every time they came to pick up their duo. Kimberly's friend, much to his mother's distress, was toying with the idea of becoming a policeman and so wanted to interrogate Robin, while Kimberly was becoming increasingly attracted to a future in television production, and Nick proved a willing target for her questions. I don't know exactly what advice was passed to either of them, as I had been deftly manoeuvred out of the room to make tea, but the would-be policeman is now studying to be a surgeon while Kimberly's resolve to become the next Louis Theroux just grew and grew. I have mixed feelings about that. While it's wonderful that she has found a career she loves, I have begun to fear that the subject of her first documentary might be living with eccentric parents in a house overrun by hordes of dogs. She certainly has the source material for it.

Some of which undoubtedly features Maxwell and Barney. Robin and Nick brought the dogs over to meet me and spent almost two hours at my house drinking tea and chasing balls. Maxwell declined to join us. She wouldn't come out of the car. She's not into socialising. Barney, however, more than makes up for it. He is, without a doubt, the friendliest dog in the world. He is also the largest animal I have ever seen without a saddle, which possibly explains why both his owners have such an enormous amount of upper body strength. He's a cross between a boxer and an Alsatian and may have inherited the wrong genes from the wrong parents. He is like two dogs joined together at the hips. The front three-quarters of him is massive, with a head that is much too far from the ground and a chest that you can't get your arms around. Where it all goes tragically wrong is when you get to his hips. Those are all Alsatian and as slim as a dancer's, and they simply can't support the front end of his body. The older Barney gets, the more out of synch the two parts of his body are becoming. His weekly hydrotherapy sessions are helping but the ultimate solution will probably have to be hip replacement surgery. I certainly hope the boys are saving up their pennies for that eventuality, although if it comes to it I am sure they can start up a collection on the Common. Everyone up there loves Barney, especially the macho guys doing fitness training. They seem to see him as a mascot. Either that or they just respect him because they know that Barney is much stronger than all of them put together.

Unfortunately Barney, the gentle giant, also has an enormous tongue and he's not afraid to use it. He loves licking people and he doesn't mind what he gets. If your hand isn't available he will settle for your trousers, or your socks, or the brand new dress that you are wearing on your way out to a party. It's not one of his better traits. What saves him is the fact that the biggest thing about him is his heart. He's not as good-looking or as cheeky as Hector, but he's completely lovable. He's like the plain friend to the really popular guy – everyone likes but him but he is so overshadowed by the other one that it takes a while for anyone to realise what a gem he is. Well, I realise it. I particularly realised it the other day when some man knocked at the door wanting to ask my opinion about something in the Book of Psalms. Barney was so desperate to go out and play with him and I was so busy trying to keep him in the house that the guy very quickly decided to give up and go away. It was wonderful. Every house needs a Barney.

His sister is of a different character entirely. She isn't as free with her affection as Barney is and makes you work for it. Perhaps it's because she's a girl named Maxwell. Apparently Nick wanted a two-syllable name beginning with 'Max' but didn't like Maxine or Maxie and so came up with Maxwell. I suppose it made sense to him at the time. Or maybe it's because she's a star and has adopted the diva mentality. You have probably seen her. She features in Nick's television commercials for a carpet cleaner and was last seen licking ice cream off a rug and tracking in mud from the garden. It must have taken a while to get those shots because she's not at all messy in real life. It would require too much effort and lack of dignity.

Maxwell has a tail like a toilet brush and an air of untouchability. She doesn't much mind people petting her but she really doesn't like being picked up. She also doesn't like thunderstorms, which makes it kind of tricky if you are trying to comfort her. During the last one, I hit upon the idea of getting down on the floor with her and putting a blanket over us. It worked fairly well and she was calming down somewhat, until her big brother thought it was a game and, after a running start, landed on top of us. I was glad my insurance payments were up to date.

I think I'm making progress with Maxie (which is what I always call her – don't tell Nick). The other day I was sitting at my desk and suddenly felt something on my foot. I looked down and was amazed to find her sitting there. I reached down to pet her but she gave me a 'don't push it' stare. So I didn't.

They may not look like siblings but Maxwell and Barney are wonderful to watch together. He spends his life rushing around like a mad thing, while she just looks at him and shakes her head. They have this big sister/little brother act down pat.

Dan

A little mischief can be endearing in many dogs, but there are one or two who might benefit from a 'time out'. Like Dan.

Hi Eileen,

Have a very nice little Jack Russell called Dan. He's nearly six, allowed on furniture and fully housetrained, although occasionally he marks his territory. He may pull on the lead but is small, doesn't fight or chew and will chase bicycles but will stop when called. Nice little dog!! Let me know if you can help.

Love

Serena x

I already knew Dan. He and I had stood outside the school gates together for years, listening to his owner tell us how clever, sporty, talented, musical and witty her children were. To be fair, she never once added the words 'than yours', but I knew they were implied. Even in a neighbourhood where competitive parenting was both a sport and an art form, Melissa stood out.

I didn't hold that against Dan, though – I had some sympathy for the fact that he had to listen to more of it than I did, living with the children and all. So I decided that I probably could help and right after school drop-off one morning, Dan arrived, walked in and immediately piddled on my sofa. Melissa was quick to point out that this was not bad behaviour or lack of housetraining; it was merely him marking his territory. My sofa and I instantly felt better.

The rest of the visit went more smoothly. Dan wandered around the garden, doing your typical dog-like things while Melissa told me a bit about her eldest son's sporting abilities (outstanding) and her middle son's artistic abilities (even more outstanding) and her youngest son's chances for a scholarship (excellent, bordering on a certainty). Eventually we started talking about the dog and she mentioned that he barks a bit but that she has a magic spray that you squirt at him which makes him stop instantly. There is nothing in the spray, it's just the puff of wind in his face that distracts him. A totally empty bottle that costs £5.99; that must have gone down a treat in the Dragons' Den. Anyway, Melissa decided that Dan would like to come and live with us inferior specimens for a while, although that isn't quite how she put it, and off they went, while I retired to bed for a little lie down.

A few days later Dan arrived, accompanied by a Melissa who was visibly trying not to cry. She felt terrible about leaving the dog while they went on holiday and even though she was sure he would be fine with me, she couldn't help but worry that he would feel abandoned. Dan, meanwhile, was playing it up for all he was worth, sitting on her lap looking mournfully at her, then at his basket and then back at her. This could have gone on for ever but luckily she had a plane to catch and so with a heavy heart and clutching a tissue, Melissa left, amid promises that not only wouldn't they be gone for long but that they would bring him back a present. Dan wasn't having any of it and hung his head in sorrow until, of course, he heard the car leave. Then he instantly perked up, ran out into the garden, did a quick circuit, barked a bit to make sure everyone was aware of his presence, came back in, wagged his tail, jumped on my lap and basically asked me what was on TV. I did feel sorry for Melissa, but you had to laugh.

Things did not remain funny for long. The problem was that Dan decided he loved me and would attack anything that came close to me. He was happiest when I was lying on the sofa and he could climb up, lie on my chest and stick his whiskers in my face. He was unhappy almost the entire rest of the time. And, when unhappy, he barked. He barked if anyone walked near me, he barked if the phone rang, he barked if it rained, he barked if a bird flew over the garden, he barked if a car came within two streets of our house, and he really barked if anyone was foolhardy enough to come anywhere near the front door. He particularly barked at the magic spray, which was rather ironic when you thought about it.

He also snarled a lot and tried to nip anything that came near him that wasn't me. Personally I didn't think he was all that bad, but it was not a popular opinion. Tom, in particular, hated him and I can't think of another dog on the planet that I can say that about. One day I walked into the kitchen and found Dan on the work surface, the microwave door open and Tom saying, 'Look inside Dan. It's really interesting in there.' I am absolutely sure that he wouldn't have microwaved the dog if I hadn't interrupted him. Really, I am. Totally sure.

Tom may have been most vocal on the subject, but he wasn't

alone in his opinions. Even people who didn't have to live with him weren't too fond of poor old Dan. A very nice lady came with her dog to visit while we had him and she asked, many times, if I could guarantee that he wouldn't be there when her little bundle of fur was with me. He was that sort of dog.

My family united behind their demands that once Dan was gone, he never be allowed back into the house. That has never happened before, or since. I felt it was harsh because he was a nice little dog, if you overlooked the constant barking, snarling and nipping. I had to tell Serena the bad news and she asked me where I thought he would be happy. After serious consideration, I decided that she needed to find a Pet Nanny who liked small, intense, yappy dogs and who lived somewhere at the end of a very long driveway that no one ever walked down or drove past. It would also be good if it was totally devoid of nature in any of its forms so that no cat/fox/bird/rabbit/insect or other dog would ever come near. Ideally she should live alone and be moderately to severely deaf. Her eyesight, however, could be perfect.

Although Dan and I had many a happy moment sitting on the sofa watching TV, in the end I wasn't sorry to see Melissa turn up to collect him. He wasn't an easy dog to have around. I think that deep down Melissa knew that Dan, unlike her children, was not perfect. But she loved him.

Alfie

Alfie is one of Christopher's favourites. The feeling is mutual. In fact, I think Alfie enjoys his stays with us more than any other guest. And why wouldn't he? Besides Christopher, there's a common at the top of the road, with a very large pond in it. That's important. Water matters to Alfie.

Hi Eileen,

I have a lovely-sounding Portuguese water dog called Alfie who is eighteen months old, not allowed on furniture, may pull a bit, doesn't moult, eats poo, loves swimming and affection and will grab your attention by hitting your leg!! Very sweet-natured, but does need grooming every day! Would you like to meet?

Love,

Sx

Would I like to meet a Portuguese water dog? Of course I would, even the poo-eating, leg-hitting variety. I've known about Portuguese water dogs since for ever. Well maybe not for ever but at least long before President Obama and his family made them fashionable. My brother (not the one with the Elvis Room and the dog named Presley, the other one) and his wife, Jane, have had Portuguese water dogs for years. Jasper and his sister Ditto are beautiful creatures with easy-going, friendly natures and an amazing amount of fur. Looking at them, it's easy to believe that the breed was originally used in the Algarve to herd fish into fishermen's nets, to retrieve broken nets or lost tackle, and to act as messengers from one ship to another. Portuguese water dogs are, quite literally, made for swimming. Their thick and curly coats are designed to stop cold water from reaching their bodies and lowering their core temperatures, so they are able to withstand whatever freezing temperatures they might find themselves in. That has come in very handy for Jasper and Ditto, since they live two paw prints away from the Atlantic Ocean and are in and out of the surf all year round. I have to admit that they aren't all that good at herding fish, but they are absolutely brilliant at retrieving tennis balls. Knowing them as I do, I wasn't overly surprised to hear that Alfie liked swimming. I just wondered where he did it.

I got to ask him a few days later when he and his owner, Francesca, came round for a visit. Alfie's family was going off to Egypt for a few weeks to lie in the sun and go swimming in the Red Sea, while poor old Alfie was staying behind to play in the garden and swim in any puddles he could find. It didn't seem fair to me, or him, but at least it meant that I got to have a water dog for a while.

Within hours of his arrival, Alfie took over the house. Everyone loved him, particularly Christopher who had, until then, always said that he wanted a Malamute when he got older. The appeal of a half-wolf, half-dog seemed to fade quickly in the face of a sweet-natured, well-behaved, very bright and enormously funny overgrown puppy. This has been a particular bonus for me, as at that point Christopher's trips home were becoming less and less frequent. Just as Kimberly was finishing her university days, Christopher was starting his, having happily swapped the quiet Kent country-side for the urban grit of Manchester. I don't think he planned his trips home around the dogs exactly, but the first question he asked whenever he was considering a visit was, 'Who are we going to have?' So when I have a dog that Christopher is particularly attached to, like Alfie, it makes a visit seem that much more likely.

Alfie loved playing, particularly with large dogs and even larger boys, and would chase sticks and balls for as long as you were willing to throw them. But while he loved his toys, his favourite possession was his blanket. He would carry it around in his mouth wherever he went. Perhaps he was pretending it was a fish or maybe a nice bit of previously lost tackle. I'm not really sure. What I am sure of is that he loved to curl up on it so that no part of his body touched the floor. Since it was only about an eighth as long or as wide as he was, that wasn't as simple as it sounds. We all spent many a happy hour watching him do this, particularly when there wasn't much on television. First he would lay his blanket down and try to spread it out with his paw. Then he would begin the serious business of circling it while he worked out his next move. This stage would last about ten minutes, during which time you could see him thinking, 'I'm sure it wasn't this small yesterday.' Then he would start crouching down as he circled, getting his back paws on the blanket first while he kept circling with his front half until he managed to get his front behind his back and he could tuck himself neatly in. I guess centuries of sleeping in coils of rope in the prow of a Portuguese fishing boat comes in handy every now and then.

While that was highly amusing, we had even more fun when walking him. Most people would tell me how beautiful my poodle was, while I would juggle explanations of his exotic background with trying to stop him from either eating poo or diving into the pond right next to the sign that told me to keep my dog out of the water. It wasn't easy.

It also wasn't easy grooming him. Thanks to Obama, you almost certainly know that Portuguese water dogs don't moult, which makes them great for people with allergies and, I suppose, for people who don't like vacuuming. But it also makes them a total nightmare to groom. Alfie was no exception. He came with an evil-looking comb and instructions that it was to be used daily to keep his coat under control. Easier said than done. Alfie may have loved attention, but not when it involved his comb. Then he would hide behind the sofa, which meant that I had to get around the front and pull while my assistant went to the back and pushed. I'm guessing those Portuguese fishermen never had this problem.

I might have been tempted to forget about the grooming until right before Francesca came home but that would never have worked because by then he would have been a giant fur ball with legs and I would have had to give him a crew cut to get it under control. She probably would have noticed that. Not only that but the whole family missed the dog so much that Francesca emailed him every night, from Egypt, to ask about his day. They would have been suspicious if he either didn't mention his comb or else pretended to like using it. They kept sending him pictures of their holiday (luckily only ones taken sitting at a table or in the hotel so that he couldn't see the Red Sea – that would have been mean) and asked him to send pictures of what he had been doing. I had to help him with that because, while he may be able to get his whole body on a blanket a fraction of his size, he is not adept at using a camera.

We may have loved Alfie, but not nearly as much as Francesca did. She was totally mad about him. Actually she was totally mad, full stop, but in a very endearing way. She treated Alfie as one of the family and always called him Alfie O'Keene or AOK for short. They were supposed to spend Christmas in Australia later that year but she couldn't bring herself to book the tickets – we were meant to be away skiing in Bulgaria at the same time and she didn't want to leave him behind with people who might not realise how wonderful he is nor, I suspect, want to spend hours of their lives uploading photos of him in red hats with white bobbles.

Happily we were both able to slightly reorganise our trips so that we were here when they were not, and vice versa. It might seem a bit over the top that we would all schedule holidays around a dog but then, you've never met Alfie.

Dylan

Christopher may have loved Alfie, and who could blame him, but one owner really took the idea of 'man's best friend' to a whole new level.

Hi Eileen,

I've got Dylan, a twenty-month-old Tibetan terrier. He plays with any dog that happens by, can pull when excited and likes to chew handbags and ladies' shoes (thin strappy leather bits are his favourite). He is very quick so requires full attention all of the time, not a big barker (actually very quiet dog), likes lots and lots of affection and loves to sit outside in the garden on his own. What do you think?

Love,

Serena

A Tibetan terrier? What is it about the dog owners in this neighbourhood and Tibet?

You probably already know this, but just in case you don't, a Tibetan terrier is an ancient breed from the remote (as opposed to the just-around-the-corner) part of Tibet, which has been developed to survive the harsh conditions, the extremes of weather and the dangerous terrain. Nomads kept them in monasteries and used them to herd and guard their animals. So a bit like Border collies, but with monks and mountains instead of flat caps and whistles.

Early one Saturday morning, Dylan braved the dangerous terrain between his side of the Common and mine. He triumphed over the pond, skirted around the ice cream van and fearlessly marched through the children's playground to arrive at my front door with Gareth in tow.

When I opened the door, I was confronted with one of the friendliest and most beautiful dogs in the world. He had long, silky, jet-black fur which would not be out of place in a shampoo commercial, springs in all four paws, a waggly feathery tail and a personality that made Tigger look a bit sedate. He immediately took to bounding around the garden, knocking over the flower pots and disturbing the wildlife with such total abandon and joyful zest that you just had to stand there and laugh.

Gareth, I couldn't help noticing, was enormous. He must easily be the tallest person in the world who does not actually play professional basketball. Perhaps that's why Dylan liked him so much; Gareth reminded him of his mountainous homeland. Looking at Gareth filling the back doorway and beaming with pride at his pet, it was obvious that the affection was mutual.

I was happy to have Dylan come and stay; only I soon learned that he wasn't really going to be staying here at all, at least not in the usual practice. He was going to be a day boy. Gareth would drop him off on his way to work every morning at 7am and pick him up twelve hours or so later on his way back home. He needed help because the lady who normally watched Dylan during the day was going on holiday and so I was to be the stand-in, the Pet Nanny's Pet Nanny, as it were.

It was a wonderful arrangement as it meant that I got to spend a great deal of time with a very funny dog. And the longer you spent with him, the funnier he became. He had so many quirks.

For example, I found it almost impossible to understand how Dylan ever got anywhere. He never seemed to move forwards. He more or less bounced straight up and down, perhaps in some deep-rooted, genetic response to the dangerous terrain in Tibet. He was not only high, he was also fast and, however he did it, he could certainly cover distances. He loved chasing anything that moved, particularly if it was carrying an ice cream, but his absolute favourite prey was women's shoes. Anyone foolhardy enough to remove them in Dylan's presence was in for trouble. He would crouch down low and stealthily creep closer and closer until he was within striking distance. Then he would suddenly pounce and be off across the Common before the barefoot victim knew what had hit her. I have to hand it to Dylan, he never went for the low end of the shoe market. Not for him your basic flip-flops or trainers. No, he specialised in expensive leather ones, preferably with straps. I'm not sure if they were easier to carry off at speed or if he just liked the look of them. Either way, it was great fun for him and good exercise for both of us. Most people took it in good humour, which yet again shows that beautiful creatures can get away with a lot of things that mere mortals can't, but there were always a few who didn't see the funny side. That never seemed to bother Dylan, certainly not enough to stop him from carrying on doing it. When you are used to routinely traversing hazardous Himalayan terrain, a few harsh words aren't likely to bother you.

Gareth came to pick Dylan up every evening and always seemed absolutely delighted to be reunited with him. In fact, I soon came to suspect that Dylan might just be the love of Gareth's life, and this despite the fact that he had a very lovely Italian girlfriend. Over the weeks I learned that Anna, for reasons which totally eluded Gareth, felt that he was more attached to the dog than he was to her. Judging from chats we had while handing over leads and treats, I'm guessing that things like cancelling their long-planned holiday at the last minute because Dylan wasn't feeling well and Gareth didn't want to leave him might have had something to do with it. Or maybe it was Gareth's decision that Anna couldn't put her clothes in the bedroom cupboard because Dylan liked sleeping in there. Or perhaps it was knowing that Dylan had a stronger claim to a spot on the two-seater sofa than she was ever going to have. Or it could have been something else entirely. I have never met Anna, so I can't possibly say.

I did wonder myself, however, why a man would have a dog that he hardly ever saw and which cost him a fortune in day care. I asked Gareth that once and he said that the weekends with Dylan made it all worth it. You only had to look at his face as he watched his dog play to realise that he meant it, and that the Italian girlfriend didn't stand a chance.

Bertie

Gareth would do anything for Dylan and, much to my horror, so would Katherine for Bertie.

Hi Eileen,

I have Bertie, a year-old cocker spaniel who will be visiting us from north London! He's fine with other dogs, doesn't fight, is a bit submissive. Not yappy, chases and retrieves a ball, loves swimming, loves affection and isn't demanding. Oh, and she may steal off the table if food is at her level! What do you think?

Sx

What I thought was – what? Why would a dog commute from the furthest reaches of north London to come stay with us? What I said was, of course I would love to meet a non-demanding, ball-retrieving, affectionate cocker spaniel, even if he was from the wrong side of the river.

Some days later and very many hours after expected, an incredibly rattled lady and her placid dog arrived. Katherine had left home over four hours earlier and had encountered traffic from pretty much the end of her road to the beginning of mine. I know we Pet Nannies are worth travelling for, but this trek across London seemed a bit ridiculous until Katherine told me a complicated tale involving a last-minute free ticket to accompany her husband on an overseas business trip to Hungary or Hamburg or Honduras or maybe it was Hawaii – I don't know but it began with an 'H' – a son who lived in Streatham and something to do with a change of cars outside Gatwick.

I don't know what she was changing her car for near the airport but the one outside my house was filled with dog things, so I quickly realised that we were not just meeting to see if we were happy with each other, she was actually handing over the dog. That was fairly unusual but so was commuting to get to me so I figured that as long as the dog was happy staying, I would be happy having her. Katherine looked relieved. I don't think she had a Plan B.

Bertie ran in and started exploring while Katherine began carrying in enough Tupperware to have a party. That was odd enough but when she started asking about my freezer capacity I began to really get worried. It turned out that I was right to do so because in the containers was Bertie's food – raw chicken wings, millions of them. Katherine had found time on her drive to stop by a Sainsbury's and wipe out their entire supply and had now relocated it to my kitchen. I thought it was a bit much to expect me to spend the next two weeks cooking chicken wings for the dog twice a day but it was actually much worse than that.

Bertie, it seems, owed his eye-catchingly shiny coat to the fact that he ate a diet that was as close to a natural one as possible. I had no idea what Katherine was talking about but figured it probably meant the kind of dog food that didn't come with a ring pull top. While I was busy thinking about where my tin opener was, she explained that Bertie ate a few chicken wings in the morning and a few more in the evenings along with a carrot or two during the day because his forebears would get their vegetable matter from the stomachs of the animals they ate. That got my attention. I looked at the chicken wings again. I looked at Katherine. I looked at Bertie. I had a terrible feeling I knew where this conversation was going. 'Please tell me,' I said, 'that these animals were coming out of a Kentucky Fried Chicken, in a bucket, with a choice of sauces.' For a second I could see Katherine wondering if her son in Streatham could have the dog after all, but she soon realised that that wasn't going to happen and so just pretended I hadn't said anything and continued to explain about how important it was that Bertie ate all of each wing, skin and bones included, and not just the 'flesh', which was the part he liked. Oh, this was going to be horrible.

Katherine then left to go wherever it was she was going and I spent the next hour or so rearranging the contents of my fridge and freezer. Bertie spent it exploring the garden, probably hunting for lunch.

Bertie, despite the absolutely vile diet, was a wonderful dog. He was very affectionate but had a cat-like sense of his own worth. He was also lively and, it has to be said, did look like he was bursting with health.

Things started to go wrong when Kimberly, a vegetarian of long standing, came downstairs the next morning, walked into the kitchen and stepped into a pile of raw chicken flesh. She let out a primeval screech worthy of an animal who was trying to protect the vegetable matter in her stomach. Everyone came running to find the kitchen floor covered in little bits of dead chicken. It was like the opening scenes of *Saving Private Ryan*, but – thankfully – with poultry. Even worse was the overpowering smell, which would undoubtedly have given Hannibal Lector an appetite but really didn't do much for us. In the midst of all this carnage sat Bertie, next to the empty Tupperware container that hadn't made it into the refrigerator the night before, since that was already crammed with as many dead chickens as it was ever going to hold. Admittedly Bertie did look pretty healthy sitting there, certainly healthier than Kimberly or the chickens.

Things didn't get any better when I went to get the broom to sweep up the mess only to discover that he had already been in the utility room and, probably in response to a primordial dietary requirement for plastic, had chewed every single one of the attachments for my brand new hoover. I started wishing that Bertie would disappear, which proves that you should always be careful of what you wish for.

A few days later, Bertie and I were alone in the house. I went outside to get something from the car, came back in, got out the chicken wings and called Bertie for dinner. No Bertie. I looked for him in the garden. No Bertie. I walked around the house. No Bertie. I looked in every room, in every cupboard, under every bed. No Bertie. I went back out into the garden, calling him in an increasingly loud voice. He was nowhere to be found. I was totally bewildered by this and then I suddenly remembered that I had gone out front to the car. I had closed the door behind me when I left so he couldn't have escaped, but then started wondering, did I? Could he?

By that point I was beginning to panic. My next-door neighbour, who had heard all the calling, came out to help. So did his wife. He got in his car to scour the neighbourhood for a runaway cocker spaniel while his wife and I scoured the Common, which is surprisingly large when you are running around it like a mad person. No one had seen the dog although everyone had seen someone else further along the path who might have. We covered every inch of the area, twice, calling until we were both hoarse. I simply couldn't understand how it had happened. Where was the dog? How was I going to explain this to Serena? Who was going to tell Katherine? It was a nightmare. Eventually we gave up and went home. My neighbour Gill from across the road passed us and I told her what had happened. She decided that we should check the garden again. So off we all went, her, me, her daughter Ellie, my neighbour Sue and her husband Grant. We called Bertie, we beat the bushes, we checked the children's treehouse, and the long-discarded sand pit. The dog was still nowhere to be found. We had no idea what to do next, but then Gill had the brilliant idea of getting her dog over, to see if he could sniff Bertie out.

I was already familiar with Gill's dog and I really wasn't sure about his bloodhound abilities but by that point I was desperate. So Mickey arrived on the scene and after two seconds, in true super-dog style, he ran over to the shed and started barking. There was a muffled reply. We got down on the ground around the shed calling for Bertie. He definitely answered, we thought. Mickey had no doubt and after a while neither did we. Bertie was definitely under the shed, in the fox hole that I had no idea was there. After another hour or so, and lots of digging, we finally got him out. He was completely and utterly unmoved by the experience and ran straight off to play with Mickey. The rest of us opened a much-needed bottle of wine.

It was a truly terrible experience and made me realise just how much responsibility you take on when you watch someone else's pet. Katherine returned a few days later and I told her what had happened. I'm not sure what I expected her to reply but it was probably something along the lines of either, 'What, you lost my dog?!' or else 'Thank you so much for rescuing my beloved Bertie', but in the end all she did say was, 'Yes, he does have a thing about foxes.' Perhaps I didn't explain the whole thing well enough.

As I saw Katherine, Bertie and all the empty Tupperware disappear up the road, I wondered how long it was going to take to recover from his visit. Between the chicken and the shed, it had been a gruelling two weeks. It was totally beyond me how anyone could deal with the stress that that dog entailed on a permanent basis. Suddenly I started suspecting that the 'H' place that Katherine had spent the past fortnight in was 'home', without Bertie or the wings. If that turned out to be true, I for one wouldn't blame her.

Would I have Bertie back again? He was a nice dog but I'm going to have to pass on this one, at least until he changes his diet and the foxes find a new home.

Abby

Education is very important. Everyone should be able to read – or at least to write. Take Abby …

Hi Eileen,

I've got Abby, a six-month-old chocolate Lab. She is a lively, well-trained dog who loves children, chasing balls, affection and going for walks. She only chews if she is bored and will do anything for food. A typical Labrador.

Love,

Serena x

The typical Labrador, her typical Labrador owner and her very sweet little baby all arrived early one morning, straight from their walk on the Common. The dog was muddy, the owner was wearing her Hunter wellies and an Alice band and the baby was fast asleep. After a bit of a palaver involving towels, paws, boots, socks and a lot of apologies about the carpet, we got ourselves sorted and went off in search of a nice cup of tea, while Abby went in search of a ball with such enthusiasm that she woke up the baby. At which point something very strange happened. Lizzie, who had up to this point seemed as normal as most of the people living in this neighbourhood, suddenly started ignoring me and from then on directed everything she had to say through baby William. As in, 'William, tell the nice lady who is going to be watching Abby that she only has one meal a day, at around 5pm' or 'William, Abby can really pull hard when she sees a squirrel, can't she?' It went on like this for ages, and started to feel a bit ridiculous. Abby thought so too. We had a little conversation about it when the two of us went into the kitchen for some water.

I guess William thought it was a good idea for Abby to stay with us, because a few evenings later she and her things arrived. It soon became apparent that Serena's description of the dog was not what it should have been. While the parts about Abby being a lovely six-month-old chocolate Lab who was well-trained, loved affection and chewed when bored were true, the part about her being a typical Labrador most certainly was not. Abby was, in fact, one of the cleverest dogs that I have ever encountered. At the top of her possessions I found a note that she had written herself, which would help me to take care of her. It included such instructions as: 'Now that I am six months old, I have learned how to control my bladder for much, much longer but I still need to go out for a short walk right before I go to bed' and 'Don't feed me anything other than my regular meals and titbits. I don't want to get fat!' and 'Please keep me on a lead near roads since I still don't understand how dangerous cars can be.' Abby not only knew what she knew, but she also knew what she didn't know, which is astonishing, especially when you consider she was still only six months old at the time.

Besides the note, she also arrived with a large rubber chicken with a squeaker in that she followed people around the house with. I kept trying, to no avail, to get her to add the lines: 'I was forced to bring this stupid chicken with me. Please hide it until I am ready to leave.' Perhaps she wasn't comfortable using a different keyboard.

Other than this extraordinary note-writing ability, Abby was indeed a typical Lab – full of bounce, with a love of chasing balls, gate-crashing picnics, jumping in puddles and just generally getting into mischief. She particularly loved being up on the Common, where she could play her favourite game of trying to catch a stick on the fly. She would start leaping as soon as she saw your arm go back and took it as a personal defeat if the stick hit the ground before she did.

She also loved playing football with boys, and the more boys the better. Happily for her, several of the local schools use the football pitches on the Common for their games lessons. You can imagine what's coming next. I tried to keep her off the field, I really did, but her eyesight was obviously better than mine because she could see a game from a long way off and would make a beeline to be part of it. She never had favourites and would happily keep the ball away from both sides. By the time I puffed my way over, you could tell which boys liked playing football and which boys didn't, just by the way they were looking at the dog. You could also tell that the teachers had really had enough of people who couldn't control their dogs, even clever dogs who could write as well as Abby could.

We thoroughly enjoyed Abby's visit, especially Tom who has a real thing about Labradors, and were sorry to see her go when the time came. Lizzie came to pick Abby up and seemed somewhat surprised when I asked if I could keep the note. But

I knew what I was doing. Anything written by such a young dog would have to be worth serious money someday.

While we waited for that day to come, I kept up with the day job, which was going through a bit of an upheaval at the time. Our lively characterful offices had caught the eye of developers and after our many years' adding to the wear on the stairs, we were given our marching orders and wound up a few miles away in a swish 'media village'. Our new surroundings came complete with studios and interview rooms and a bistro café. Not to mention the foosball and pool tables. There was a radio station next door, a television station or two upstairs and a modelling agency, with models, based as far from the café as is possible in a building that size. The people were also swish, with nice suits, high heels and sunglasses. As you can imagine, the dogs did not fit in. Neither, it must be said, did I. I started working from home whenever we had a dog to stay and I began to find it harder and harder to go in, even when we didn't have a furry guest who needed my company. I was beginning to wonder if my 'side' job was becoming more important to me than my 'main' job.

Marty

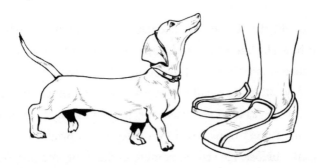

Abby might have been the smartest dog on the block, but Marty was without doubt the longest.

I have Marty, who is a two-year-old standard dachshund. May pull on the lead, doesn't fight, will chew if bored and things are 'hanging around', likes his food but isn't greedy, does bark! Loves playing with other dogs but he keeps an eye on the owner, will chase birds and squirrels, likes affection but is quite independent. What do you think?
Serena x

I thought that I knew what dachshunds looked like, which was basically like Simon and Roux, but obviously I was wrong because when Marty and his South African owner arrived a few days after the email did, it was a bit of a shock. He was about twice as high as I was expecting and easily four times as long. I don't think I had ever seen such a bizarre-looking creature before. He started coming in the door, and just kept coming. In fact he and Peta May began entering at the same time but she was halfway through telling me about how she used to live around the corner before his tail even started to appear.

Things didn't get off to a great start. For one thing, Marty sat down next to his owner and wouldn't budge. He wasn't interested in the garden, he didn't want to play with the ball I had given him, he ignored the treat and, worst of all, he wouldn't let me pet him. How could a dog not want me to pet him? When you added in his reputation for chewing things that were left hanging around, I nearly said no since most things in my house are left hanging around at some point or other. But Peta May was desperate. They were due to fly to South Africa in two days to go to her brother's wedding to Nelson Mandela's granddaughter, or her husband's brother to Nelson Mandela's lawyer's granddaughter, or someone Nelson Mandela had once passed in the street's brother to someone else's granddaughter. The words 'brother', 'wedding', 'Nelson Mandela' and 'granddaughter' all definitely figured in the story. I'm sure it wasn't that complicated but to tell the truth, I was a little distracted trying to figure out if she and Marty were currently sitting in my house drinking tea and ignoring me, respectively, because she had left finding a place for the dog to stay till the last minute, or if I was the hundredth person she had tried and the ninety-nine before me knew something I didn't. Marty wasn't saying but the look he was giving me made me slightly suspicious. In the end, I figured that it was only for two weeks, it would probably be good for us to have an incentive to stop letting things lie around, and that if Marty came to live with us I was sure I could win him over. So we decided to give it a go.

And give it a go we did. Marty came back the next day and it was obviously not only against his better judgement, but also against his will. He was not happy about being left behind. He didn't actually tell me that but I could guess by the way he made a wild dash for the door as Peta May was going out of it. When he couldn't get to her he sat there and whined and whimpered and attacked the paintwork. It was heartbreaking. The last time I experienced anything even remotely approaching it was when I left Christopher at nursery school, but without the scratching on the door. Peta May was probably not even at the top of the road and I was already regretting this decision.

But we were stuck with each other for the next fourteen days, and we were both going to have to make the best of it. We went for a walk up on the Common. I have discovered that this is the solution to most doggy problems. Besides, even if it didn't completely cheer him up, at least it would save my paintwork.

Marty was great up there. He played with everyone, he chased squirrels, he thought about fetching a ball and eventually he started looking a bit less like a broken-hearted, abandoned dog. By the time we came home, he was actually wagging his tail a little bit and not scowling at me quite so much. Result.

Despite the inauspicious beginning, Marty settled in. His reputation for chewing turned out to be ill-founded, although the one for barking certainly wasn't. He was a strange dog, though, and seemed to bark when the mood struck him rather than at anyone or anything in particular. The postman, bin man, milkman and foxes were all perfectly safe from attack, whereas an innocent-looking old lady probably had years taken off her life. She had the misfortune to walk by the front of the house at the wrong moment and next thing she knew, a barking, snarling, long dog was hurling himself at the window to get to her. Thank goodness for double glazing.

Marty soon warmed to me. Actually he got boiling hot. Instead of ignoring me, he started following me around, endlessly. I would wake up in the morning and find that he had made his way upstairs during the night and was sleeping next to my side of the bed. I would come out of the shower to find him lying on my towel. He would sit on my foot during breakfast. It continued like that, all day long. Wherever I was, Marty was. He was obviously a one-person dog, and that person was me. Christopher tried to make friends. He was the chief dog walker and while Marty certainly enjoyed his time up on the Common, he treated Christopher like staff. He didn't mind sitting at Christopher's feet and watching rugby on TV, especially if South Africa was playing, but he would growl at any attempt to pet him. Christopher took the hint and stopped trying. But that wasn't good enough for Marty. He didn't want Christopher anywhere near me and would growl and snap at him if ever he came too close. Unfortunately too close in Marty's mind was anywhere in the same room, which got tricky at mealtimes. Tom, meanwhile, was convinced that he could win Marty over and every evening would track him down, trap him and make the dog sit on the sofa with him. This worked until the second Tom let him go. Then Marty would instantly leap off, run over to sit next to me and give Tom his signature look. I'm not sure that the 'track and trap' method was really such a good idea, but I doubt anything else would have worked much better. Marty wasn't having any of it. It was me, or no one.

So that's how we spent the following days. I was in constant danger of tripping over the ridiculously long dog every time I took a step. Tom's feelings were constantly being hurt and Christopher gave up, kept his distance and pocketed his dog walker's fee. Kimberly, meanwhile, stayed at work until it was safe to come home.

I have to say that I not-so-secretly enjoyed the fact that Marty liked me best but I wasn't entirely convinced by his change of heart. Not only was it too extreme, but I also couldn't forget that it wasn't all that long ago when I was on the receiving end of those looks. Now, just a few days after he wouldn't even let me pet him, Marty was apparently perfectly happy to live with me for ever. I suspected that as soon as Peta May came back from seeing, or not seeing, Nelson Mandela, Marty would forget me in an instant. It wasn't so much that he was fickle as that he was serially, obsessively devoted. If dogs had mottos, his would undoubtedly have been, 'If you can't be with the one you love, love the one you're with.'

After a while, though, Marty thawed slightly towards the rest of the household and by the time he left we all thought that Marty was a lovable, if somewhat odd, little chap (except Christopher, who never forgave him for rooting for South Africa). Aside from his unique looks and ways, he had many good qualities – he didn't climb into the dishwasher to lick plates, for example. He also came when called, if he happened to be ready to come when he was called. And with absolutely no thought to his own personal safety, he was prepared to protect the house fearlessly from any and all little- to medium-sized old ladies.

While there may have been many drawbacks to living with Marty, the biggest problem wasn't his fault. I blame it firmly on the 1990s pop group Aqua. For his entire stay, and for a substantial amount of time afterwards, we all wandered around the house speaking in fake Californian accents and singing, *'Come on Marty, let's go party. Hah, hah, hah, yeah.'* I've got it going around in my head just thinking about him.

The wedding, by the way, was apparently wonderful but I never did figure out the Nelson Mandela connection. I was too busy trying not to be upset that Marty had totally deserted me the second Peta May turned up at the door. I knew he would, but that didn't make me feel any better when he did.

I didn't have much time to brood over Marty's fickle affections, however. The continuing conflict between my Pet Nanny lifestyle and our new office surroundings in the media village finally pushed us to make a decision – much like the children growing up, change had been forced upon us. A change that we didn't particularly like. It was time for a rethink. It was time to move on. We sold the company we had founded the year Kimberly was born, we handed the keys over to the new owner and we set up two offices at home. Tom got the one upstairs, from which he launched LookAhead TV, a bold new venture in programming, while I spread out downstairs and got seriously into my new life as a writer and dedicated Pet Nanny, and I haven't looked back since.

A Dog for All Occasions

People often ask me if I've ever thought of going back to my pre-Serena life, when the house was our own and we weren't tripping over four-footed guests. 'Don't you ever wish you could sleep late and not have to look after other people's pets?' they ask. 'Don't you miss being a diplomat?'

I'm not sure they believe me when I say I don't – the experience was right for me at the time, and I have many happy memories, but truthfully my current lifestyle suits me much better. That said, the occasional change of pace is always welcome, and the London 2012 Olympics provided a perfect opportunity. For an entire month I was back serving as a diplomat, of sorts, handling protocol for the Olympic table tennis games. Drawing on my career in the Foreign Service, I had the distinct pleasure of working with not only the sport's greatest athletes, but also members of the International Olympics Committee and International Table Tennis Federation, as well as the heads of state and government who had come to cheer their compatriots on. It was a fascinating experience and more challenging than you might expect.

I had told Serena that housing Olympic houseguests made it impossible for me to care for any canine during the games. It would be the first time since Gaby died that we would remain dogless for weeks. But serving as an Olympic volunteer and returning home exhausted each night left me no time to feel lonely – and in any case the dogs had been replaced by a record number of humans, a dozen of them living under our roof, with two more sleeping in a garden tent.

Unlike dogs, it became clear that you had to chat with all these people, even when you were too shattered to do so. They required meals that involved much more than mystery meat in a tin along with a few biscuits. The humans did not bring their own beds, pillows or blankets, all of which had to be provided. None came with their own toys. There was also a certain reduced access to the shower. The dogs never queued up for the coffee-making facilities, or chatted you up at the breakfast table when you needed to be heading out the door to keep the table tennis games on schedule.

There were, of course, some advantages to caring for humans. For one thing, they didn't devour raw chicken wings or tear at the antique rug. Generally they would laugh at our jokes and not piddle on the upholstery. And they kept the wine store nicely stocked.

Overall the fact that these people were more articulate than our normal visitors made up for the greater lack of privacy. The house was filled with the sounds of guests reliving their Olympic experiences, with tales of Centre Court at

Wimbledon, of clashes on the handball and basketball courts. We discussed why men liked boxing and women did not, argued about whether dressage was a sport or 'horse ballet', and debated whether it was necessary for women to wear tiny bikinis while playing beach volleyball. We also marvelled at the amazing atmosphere you ran into everywhere you went and wondered if everyone had been infected by the most benign of viruses. We enjoyed being at home for this once-in-a-lifetime London event.

During those Olympic weeks, everyone asked what had happened to the dogs. Our friends and family were not used to visiting the house without at least one or two furry friends in attendance.

I wasn't really used to it either and while volunteering was a welcome change, I didn't have many regrets about ushering out the athletes and welcoming back the dogs. Even though we don't have one of our own, I couldn't imagine not having a constant stream of canine visitors – especially at certain festive times of year, when the presence of a dog or three can add so much entertainment value to a holiday.

There's a saying here in England: a dog is for life, not just for Christmas. I suppose it means that when you put an adorable little puppy under the tree, you have to realise that by the following year he will be large enough to jump up on the table and eat his way through three-quarters of the turkey before anyone can stop him. I know, it seems fairly obvious to me, too, but you would be shocked by the number of people who wake up in the weeks and months after Christmas and are surprised to notice that little Fido is growing up alarmingly quickly. And that's when the problems begin.

But not if you're a Pet Nanny, because we get the best of all possible worlds. Their size doesn't change much during the time they stay with us, so there are no sudden surprises when Rafa can reach the chicken defrosting on the draining board. Lily doesn't suddenly get old and become unable to manage the wooden floors. And Roux doesn't wake up one morning and decide out of the blue that he now loves rummaging through the rubbish. No, we pretty much know what we are going to get. And we know when we are going to get it.

Despite the fact that we haven't had a dog of our own since Gaby left us, we haven't had to spend a single holiday on our own for ages. Much to our friend Neil's regret – he celebrates Christmas with us most years, but suffers from allergies and I don't think he has ever really reconciled himself to having to share the day with our dog guests. For the past several years Simon and Roux, the little Texan dachshunds, have also spent the holiday with us. Roux, the trash bandit, loves turning piles of wrapping paper into confetti. I'm not sure if he is looking for food or if he just thinks you should always be prepared for a party, one at which confetti is required. His brother, Simon, loves sleeping inside his Christmas stocking, usually with his back half hanging out. Actually he likes sleeping inside any Christmas stocking, not just his own, but we have been working on that. I think he's beginning to realise that the one with the big 'S' on it is his but just to be certain, we have started hanging everyone else's up higher. That seems to work.

Rafa, the labradoodle, enjoys Thanksgiving. He not only likes the buzz of the house getting ready, but he really loves it when the food starts being prepared. His nose is all over the place, although his favourite spot is sitting in front of the oven, staring at the turkey as it cooks. He would obviously prefer it to be squirrel, but he's willing to compromise. He also likes hiding under the table at dinnertime, which isn't easy considering his size. He spends the whole meal making his way from one end to the other, and back again. You can always tell where he is because you see people's hands going down under the tablecloth, one by one. Like a Mexican wave but in reverse, and with turkey. Not everyone enjoys his presence, though. Our friend David says it's not that he doesn't like dogs; it's just that he isn't too fond of suddenly being hit with a wet nose. Especially when he is minding his own business, eating his Thanksgiving dinner. I suppose it takes all kinds.

Elvis and Vegas are fiends for Halloween. Literally. Fiends. I should probably tell you that Halloween is the highlight of the year for Tom. Yes, I think it's a little bit strange too, but there you have it. Tom starts preparing from around mid-November of the year before. By the day itself he has his costume, his background music, his props and enough goodies to set up his own sweet shop. He has played several characters over the years, Dracula being one of my favourites, but he seems to have settled on Quasimodo recently. He has sewn a pillow into an old sweater, which serves as a hump, wears a tatty wig, a few nasty moles and heavy boots. When the doorbell goes he cues the eerie music, opens the creaky door, grabs the silver candelabra in one hand, the container of sweets in the other, and scares the life out of whoever is on the other side.

This is where Elvis and Vegas come in. They are stationed in the front room, overlooking the doorway, and as they hear the words, 'Would you like a sweetie', they leap into action and start barking wildly at the window. This, I must say, is seriously terrifying since Elvis looks mean, what with those Kaiser Wilhelm eyebrows and that steely stare, and Vegas looks fat enough to have eaten the last few children who dared to come by. Between Quasimodo in one direction and the hounds from hell in the other, the poor child has nowhere to go. Tom thought he had reached the heights of success this year when one little girl was so terrified that she wet herself. Luckily her father thought it was hilarious but I predict a law suit in the future, and very expensive therapy bills. That's really something to be frightened of. Tom, meanwhile, is more concerned about Elvis and Vegas not making it for Halloween next year and wants me to book them in with their owner. I'm not sure how that conversation would go: 'Can I have your scary and fat dogs so my husband can use them to terrify small children?' Hmmm, I may have to work on that.

If it's Easter, it must be Lily. She's a thousand years old, and of very mixed ancestry. I always thought she was just an odd-looking Labrador, but apparently that's one of the very few things she isn't. Her family has a house in Menorca, lucky devils, and spends Easter there every year. Apparently that's the best time to be in Spain. I wouldn't know about that, but I do know that Easter is a great time to have Lily. A lot of other dogs might make the annual Easter egg hunt a bit difficult to set up, unless you were willing to hide one egg as the previous one was being found, but not Lily. She's not a big fan of chocolate, or of moving too much, so you could hide one in her basket the night before and still be confident that the clue 'Where you are most likely to find an Easter flower' will eventually have the hunter collecting the prize. She's also great in another important way. Because she's so arthritic, she needs to be taken for long walks to make sure that her joints don't completely seize up. But because she's so old, she walks slowly, very slowly. The combination makes her perfect for the post-lunch, ate-too-many-chocolates stroll around the Common. By that point, everyone else needs to walk too, and no one can do it very quickly.

Of course there are holidays when it's good to know what dog not to have. Guy Fawkes Night and Maxwell, for example, do not go together. She gets nervous when a car door slams too loudly, so having the entire sky suddenly light up with fireworks is beyond her ability to cope with. It's best to avoid Pepe on the 4th of July. Being a saluki/greyhound, he's just the right height and speed for getting the hot dogs off the barbecue before you can stop him, although he can be left safely with corn on the cob for hours. And you would never have Dylan on Valentine's Day. Not that he wouldn't be a lovely addition to the day, it's just that his owner loves him too much to leave him then, no matter how many times his girlfriend hints about romantic getaways to Paris.

Being a Pet Nanny means that a dog really isn't just for Christmas, he's for lots of different holidays. And of course, he's lots of different dogs. As I said, the best of all possible worlds.

Even so, many of our friends still worry that Tom and I can't live happily ever after without a dog to replace Gaby. They keep asking, 'When are you going to get another dog of your own?'

I tried to explain why that would never happen. My profession is a bit like being a grandparent and having the kids come to stay. They are always glad to play with you and it's a pleasure to spoil them a bit. Fortunately the ultimate responsibility lies elsewhere and it is wonderful to hand them back, pour a glass of wine and know that all behaviour problems are back in the hands of their owners.

The one exception, however, is Rafa. There's something special about him. Perhaps it's his unbounded enthusiasm for life, his unquenchable optimism, his ability to make any day seem a better one for having spent it with him. Maybe he simply knows that deep down I really wish he was my dog. I know I can trust you with my secret. If all goes terribly wrong for his very nice owners, someday he may be. They have, after all, named me his guardian in their will, despite the fact that each of their three grown-up sons wanted the job ahead of me. Naturally, they lost. I can assure you, however, that in the unlikely event that Rafa does move into our house, the boys will still see plenty of their beloved dog. After all, I would need a Pet Nanny from time to time.

But for now, we're happy as things are. It has been an exciting journey from American diplomat to British Pet Nanny, with its ups and downs, its triumphs and occasional disasters, its moments of happiness, and some of sadness. And, of course, its many, many dogs.

Biographies

HECTOR

Born in 2006 in Essex, Hector is known for his poor food choices. This habit started early in life when he ate some of the amniotic sac in which he had entered the world, and has led to numerous health problems over the years. Still, our favourite Weimaraner never lets a few rashes or upset tummies slow him down. True to his roots as a royal huntsman, he loves chasing anything that moves and will make do with squirrels if wild boar is not available. Sleek, attractive and intelligent, Hector and his fellow Weimaraners need a lot of exercise, plenty of space and a firm but gentle hand for them to thrive. About twenty-four inches high, seventy pounds heavy and with a tendency to knock things over, he may not be the right pet for a young family but if you have time and space to give him, and some serious upper body strength, a Weimaraner could be just the dog for you.

VITA

Born in Devon in 2008, Vita hails from canine aristocracy. Her grandfather was a Crufts champion and Vita has certainly inherited his style and beauty. Her mischievousness and love of chewing, however, are all her own. Originally from central Europe, the Pomeranian may look like a pampered pooch but beneath that fluffy exterior lies the heart of a true mischief-maker. Descended from large working dogs in the Arctic regions, today's Pomeranian is somewhat smaller but is at home in any setting, be it urban, suburban or rural. About ten inches tall and five pounds heavy, Vita and her fellow Pomeranians are friendly and lively, and their size makes them suitable for families of all kinds. If you like happy, self-confident and endearing dogs, a Pomeranian would certainly fit your bill. Just make sure you keep wallets and wires out of sight. She has been known to mistake them for vermin.

RAFA

Born in Northampton in 2008, Rafa is known for his unbounded enthusiasm for life, for his enormous heart and for his even bigger body. Rafa took to obedience training with his usual gusto and can respond to whistles, prance like a pony and sit upon command – but only when he wants to. Like all labradoodles, he combines the Labrador's loving nature with the poodle's sense of his own self-worth. Intelligent, energetic and allergen-friendly, labradoodles come in all shapes and sizes. Rafa's size is off the chart, enabling him to reach absolutely every counter in any kitchen, a slight problem when it comes to any attempt to defrost a chicken. Rafa's favourite hobby is chasing squirrels and his favourite place is right by your side.

ELLA

Born in Surrey in 2007, Ella is friendly, affectionate, good-natured, easy-going and gentle. She is also much calmer than your average Labrador. She loves going for slow walks, her stuffed toy Duckie and people. She is also exceedingly fond of food, which could explain why she is always on a diet. Ella enjoys being part of a crowd but, unlike other Labs, she rarely feels the need to fetch, chase or retrieve. At sixty-five pounds in weight and only twenty-two inches high, she could definitely stand to lose some weight, although she's not letting an extra pound or two interfere with her enjoyment of life.

ELVIS AND VEGAS

Born in Manchester in 2003, Elvis was joined by sister Vegas the following year. Looking like a younger, leaner, more canine version of the late Kaiser Wilhelm, Elvis carries himself with a distinctive military bearing. Vegas, meanwhile, is softer and, well, rounder. Both, however, have the typical miniature schnauzer's square, sturdy frame and bushy eyebrows, whiskers and chin. Like most of their breed, Elvis and Vegas are alert, intelligent and very playful. Originally bred to chase rats from German barns, they now spend much of their time keeping the garden safe from hedgehogs. They are fearless and tend to rush into situations that other, more prudent, dogs might walk away from. Elvis is about fourteen inches high and weighs about sixteen pounds. Vegas is shorter and heavier. I'll leave it at that. They both love getting lots of attention and enjoy spending their spare time protecting their turf and going for walks. Dogs like this perfect pair are ideal pets for anyone who wants a friendly, bright and playful companion – and is willing to spend a lot of time explaining to the small boys in the neighbourhood that the ball that just came sailing over the fence, is no more.

HARRISON

Born in Suffolk in 2003, Harrison has spent most of the time since then pursuing his favourite hobby – growing. He could generally be described as 'enormous', at twenty-six inches in height and tipping the scale at over seventy-five pounds. Like other Chesapeake Bay retrievers, Harrison loves swimming and is never happier than when retrieving downed birds from icy water. This pastime is probably easier to indulge in his native eastern Maryland than it is on Wandsworth Common, but he is always willing to give the swans up there a good run for their money. He is loving, friendly and willing to please but he also has a tendency to think that he is the boss. Firm handling, lots of exercise and a small pond are all he needs to be in heaven.

BUSTER

Born in Oxfordshire in 2007, Buster has a face that only a near-sighted mother could love. Long, thin, with an overly long snout, slightly crossed eyes and unruly ears, his visage might not win him beauty contests but his personality certainly wins him hearts. Buster, like all other collies, is a natural herder and loves making sure that everyone is within his sight. This, of course, can be a bit of a problem, unless everyone agrees to co-operate with his plan, at all times. He is intelligent, sweet-natured and loyal, but gets easily bored and needs regular, long walks. At twenty-five inches high and sixty-five pounds heavy, he's big but not particularly strong and his lovely temperament makes him good with children, despite his occasionally eccentric behaviour.

COCO AND ALASKA

Born in Somerset in 2006, Coco now lives in London with her niece, Alaska. The two years' difference in age, however, is not apparent and the 'girls' are almost impossible to tell apart. Both less than a foot tall and a dozen pounds heavy with lovely white fur, they are typical West Highland terriers. They are small, compact and full of character. Like most Westies, the girls are extraordinarily friendly and love being part of a family. They enjoy chasing cats but would have no idea what to do next if they caught one, and will often bark just for the sheer fun of it.

BABS

Born in London in 2008, Babs loves sitting in fruit bowls and sleeping in the deep pocket of a large hoodie. Being a miniature dachshund means that she is only six inches high, about eight pounds heavy and longer than she is tall. Lively, affectionate and fun to have around, Babs is happiest when allowed to burrow and her main hobby is trying to make friends with the little dog she keeps meeting in the mirror.

JESSIE

Born in Kent in 2008, Jessie has all the makings of a really nice dog. She is playful, good-natured and gets on well with everyone she meets. Sadly she has never been able to recognise valuable household items such as, for example, an antique Chinese rug. A wheaten terrier, Jessie's antecedents are thought to go back over 2,000 years. They originated first in Ireland, were primarily used to rid farmland of vermin, and are generally graceful, strong and sporty dogs. With that background, it should come as no surprise that she is bold, inquisitive and always ready for action. Unfortunately the action in our case was chewing. Still, with a bit of training and a lot of affection she will undoubtedly make a wonderful family pet.

ROUX AND SIMON

Born in the USA in 2001, Roux was joined by brother Simon four years later. While Roux is often plagued by problems brought on by his uncontrollable love of food, Simon is characterised by his need to be loved. Neither is bigger than seven inches high or heavier than a large bag of potatoes, but they both take up an enormous amount of space in the heart of anyone who meets them. Their dachshund heritage makes them excellent burrowers and their Texan background ensures their love of American football. Perhaps spending their formative years in a drier climate than London's could explain their reluctance to go for walks in the rain. Or it may just be down to their superior intelligence. Affectionate, brave and loving, no Christmas is complete without them.

RUBY

Born in south London in 2001, Ruby is known for her beautiful brown eyes and her supermodel attitude. Just ten inches high and ten pounds heavy, she is a hardy little dog with a spirited, lively personality and a bark she isn't afraid to use when protecting her people and her home. It comes as no surprise that her Lhasa apso ancestors hail from Tibet and were originally used as watchdogs in the country's sacred temples and monasteries. Ruby wouldn't mind living in a flat, as long as she gets her daily walk, and would make a great pet for anyone with a bit of space and a lot of love to spare. She would be especially happy with someone who enjoyed brushing her coat on a regular basis; an ability to put in bows is optional.

JACKSON

Born in Oxfordshire in 2010, Jackson's grasp of English is not all that it could be and he prefers conversing in either Spanish or Greenlandic. Despite his exotic home life, Jackson is just your typical retriever – loyal, affectionate and willing to please. In whatever language you want to say it, he is the perfect family pet. Just don't leave the bathroom door open while having a soak unless you want company in the tub.

BARNEY AND MAXWELL

Born in 2006, Barney is a natural little brother. With the powerful build of his boxer father, combined with the good-natured loyalty of his Alsatian mother, he is tall, strong and playful. Barney's greatest love in life is finding a puddle to roll in. His greatest irritant is his little, big sister. Born in 2002, Maxwell may be a fraction of Barney's size but she knows how to keep him under her paw. Her Lakeland terrier ancestors may have been used to prevent foxes from destroying the crops but Maxwell turns all her terrier talents into making sure her big, little brother knows his place. They may not immediately look like a natural pairing, but they really are a perfect match.

DAN

Born in Yorkshire in 2004, Dan's favourite hobbies are barking and digging. A small, intense dog with a lot of energy, he is all Jack Russell and it is not at all difficult to believe that his forebears were used in fox hunting. In fact, no fox dared show its snout in our garden while Dan was in charge; neither did little old ladies or cyclists, who either dismounted fast or pedalled even faster. About nine inches high and twelve pounds heavy, Norfolks are courageous, affectionate and, above all, energetic. They make great family pets, but be prepared to spend a lot of your time throwing balls and apologising to strangers.

ALFIE

Born in Dorset in 2007, Alfie spends his spare time looking for a puddle to jump into and for a stick to retrieve. If he can find the two at the same time, he's ecstatic. Like most Portuguese water dogs, Alfie is lively, loyal and simply great to be around. At twenty-two inches high and fifty pounds in weight, Alfie can be quite a handful if he feels you are not walking fast enough on the way to the Common. But a few tugs on the lead usually let him know who's setting the pace. His affectionate nature and fun-loving ways make him a great family pet. They also make him hard to hand back to his owners when his holiday with us is over.

DYLAN

Born in 2009 in Surrey, Dylan's main aims in life are to look beautiful and to have fun. With gloriously silky fur, jet engines in all four paws and an unquenchable enthusiasm for life, he lights up the day for anyone he meets. Over 2,000 years ago, his ancestors were kept as good luck charms by Tibetan monks and it was pure luck that brought this Tibetan terrier bounding to our door. Like others of his breed, Dylan is lively, gentle and very agile. He loves herding, running and being the centre of attention. At seventeen inches high and thirty pounds in weight, Dylan needs a lot of exercise and constant praise. He is a wonderful family pet, as long as he understands that everyone, including the children, are his pack leaders. Dylan and his fellow Tibetan terriers need a lot of grooming but then beauty on this level usually requires high maintenance.

BERTIE

Born in north London in 2010, Bertie is a credit to his diet. Bright eyes, a glossy coat and an overall air of health show what a 'natural' way of eating can accomplish. Friendly, energetic, willing and obedient, Bertie and his fellow cocker spaniels are the ideal human companions. Affectionate, good-natured and sincere, this dog loves everyone – except foxes. Originally bred to flush out and spring on game, Bertie's attempts at pursuing such practices tend to result in his getting stuck down foxholes. At twenty inches high and fifty pounds in weight, he fits into any home as long as he has lots of opportunities to run off some energy.

ABBY

Born in Devon in 2012, Abby is just your basic Labrador. That is, of course, if you picture your Lab with a glorious velvety brown coat and an enviable ability to express herself in writing. When not composing lists, Abby loves nothing more than chasing balls, rolling in mud and running off with someone else's picnic. She also, for reasons she has never bothered to commit to paper, has a strong affection for an exceptionally noisy rubber chicken. Despite her many talents, Abby has never developed a diva personality and remains a down-to-earth, enthusiastic and totally lovable Lab.

MARTY

Born in Essex in 2010, Marty is an unusual-looking creature. Some eleven inches high, he is easily twice that in length so watching him enter a room is a wonderful experience. Like other standard dachshunds, his roots go back to sixteenth-century Germany where his antecedents were bred to hunt small game. His short legs and courageous nature meant he could follow rabbits and badgers into their lairs. That skill is less useful in twenty-first century London, but Marty still loves burrowing and can often be found with his head buried deep into any pile of laundry that he happens to encounter. While he might like jumping on sofas and beds, he has to be discouraged from doing so since his long back really doesn't take well to such strenuous activities.

TOM

Born in Washington DC in 1949, Tom is from a military family and grew up in Army bases around the world and across the southern USA. This experience has left him with a life-long inability to shut windows or lock doors. His grandfather's observation that he would make a great general but would be court-martialled before he could get there, turned Tom away from the family business and towards journalism. After moving to Britain as a young man, Tom spent years as a diplomatic correspondent before starting up his own company. He is now CEO of LookAhead TV. Tall, bald, one-eyed and with a limp, Tom is totally incapable of being embarrassed by anything and has an inexhaustible supply of optimism which he rolls out in all situations, even those in which optimism is decidedly not called for. Tom loves his family, his work and dogs of all sizes. His hobbies are history, Scouting and telling the same stories, over and over again.

EILEEN

Born in New York longer ago than she cares to think about, Eileen was a diplomat before becoming a Pet Nanny. She lives in London with husband Tom, children Kimberly and Christopher, and an insane number of other people's animals. In her spare time, she is an editor and a director at LookAhead TV and, as she never tires of telling people, was a Games Maker at the London 2012 Olympics. Her hobbies include playing the flute badly, cycling slowly, and eating enormous amounts of ice cream. She also likes dogs, and writing.

Acknowledgements

Since I have been talking about writing a book for a very long time now, there are a lot of people to thank for having given me the support and encouragement I needed to get here: my family, friends, colleagues, neighbours, acquaintances and basically everyone I have ever sat next to on a long-haul flight. Thank you to all of them. But especially to:

My brothers and their wives, Jimmy & Jane Riley and Dennis & Ann Riley, for being part of my story from the first page to the last. And for remembering why we named our dog McTavish. Who else could I have asked? And also to Jimmy for his sage legal advice.

Bob Arms for his perseverance in asking for the first chapter of my book for Christmas, year after year after year.

Carla Rapoport and Harriet Cohen for their non-stop encouragement, advice, and, it must be said, nagging. They made me keep going, even when I didn't think I could.

Roger Rapoport for all his hard work with the initial editing and for seeing what the book could be.

John Marquis, Imogen Graham, Kate Cheshire and Laura Davies for reading the early drafts and never, not once, telling me to give up.

Adam and Roxana Lovick for their unfailing encouragement, interest and help. But mostly for letting me pretend that Rafa is my dog.

Serena Perkins, the Chief Pet Nanny, without whom there would be no story to tell.

Beth Colocci for making the author's photo shoot, if not an enjoyable experience, at least a bearable one.

Everyone at Elliott & Thompson, especially Olivia Bays and Pippa Crane, for guiding me through the mysterious world of publishing.

My children, Kimberly and Christopher Arms, for letting me turn them into characters in my book. And for never doubting that I could do it.

My husband, Tom Arms, fellow Pet Nanny and partner in all things. For everything.

And finally, to all the dogs and their owners, a weirder or more wonderful group it would be hard to imagine.